PERCY BYSSHE SHELLEY

The Esdaile Poems

Oxford University Press, Ely House, London W.1

GLASGOW NEW YORK TORONTO MELBOURNE WELLINGTON
CAPE TOWN SALISBURY IBADAN NAIROBI LUSAKA ADDIS ABABA
BOMBAY CALCUTTA MADRAS KARACHI LAHORE DACCA
KUALA LUMPUR HONG KONG

The Retrospect.
Cwm Elan 1812

To trace Duration's lone career
To check the chariot of the year
Whose burning wheels forever sweep
The boundaries of oblivion's deep ....
To snatch from Time the monsters jaw
The children which she just had borne
And ere entombed within her maw
To drag them to the light of morn
And mark each feature with an eye
Of cold & pearless scrutiny ....
It asks a soul not formed to feel
An eye of glass, a hand of steel;
Thoughts that have passed thoughts that
With truth and feeling to compare;
A scene which wildered fancy viewed
In the souls coldest solitude,
With that same scene when peaceful love
Flings rapture's colour on the grove
When mountain meadow wood & stream

Shelley's transcript, in the Esdaile Notebook, of No. 50, 1–19. (*See p. 102*)

PERCY BYSSHE SHELLEY

———

The Esdaile Poems

EARLY MINOR POEMS FROM THE
'ESDAILE NOTEBOOK'

Edited from the manuscripts
with introduction, commentary, and notes
by

NEVILLE ROGERS

OXFORD
AT THE CLARENDON PRESS
1966

PRINTED IN GREAT BRITAIN
AT THE UNIVERSITY PRESS, OXFORD
BY VIVIAN RIDLER
PRINTER TO THE UNIVERSITY

IN MEMORIAM

CARISSIMAE MATRIS

QUAM TEGIT

IN COMITATU ANGULUS ILLE SUSSEX

MUSIS IPSIQUE POETAE

EXOPTATISSIMUS

PREFACE

No apology, I think, need be offered for giving to the first critically edited text of these *juvenilia* the separate publication which Shelley intended them to have. He himself had no very high opinion of them, and the modern reader is unlikely to have a higher one; nevertheless the συνετοί whom he had in mind may yet find some enjoyment in looking among them for the seeds of things to come.

A word is due on the distinction between an edited text, on the one hand, and a transcription, or modified transcription,[1] on the other. Today many more of Shelley's manuscripts are available than formerly and many more eyes may work on them. A happy result has been the recent improvement in standards of mechanical accuracy and the printing of some magnificent transcription. Less happy, however, is an increasingly fashionable tendency towards mechanical thinking, whereby transcribed material, valuable as a basis for editing, has come to be regarded as editing itself. The gulf between mere transcription and editing proper is as wide as the gulf between Shelley's poems as they appear in his manuscripts and the form in which he, or any printer of his day, would have expected them to reach their readers. Today's faith in the sufficiency of 'the manuscript'—an anxious fundamentalism now commonly called both 'modern' and 'scholarly'—is, in fact, merely a recrudescence in English studies of the old, fallacious faith in 'the best manuscript'—similarly called *eine streng wissenschaftliche Methode*—which A. E. Housman castigated so long and so wittily among editors of classical texts.

The single skill of transcribing Shelley's manuscripts is in itself so notoriously difficult that the many difficulties lying

---

[1] I have silently emended in the present volume certain modified transcriptions from the Esdaile poems which were made for the purposes of *Shelley at Work*.

beyond it can frequently become obscured. A point too easily
ignored today is that, like Milton and not a few others, Shelley
neither thought nor wrote as a monoglot man does. Style and
meaning are fused in his wonderful, fluent, classical syntax,
the power of which begins to be perceptible even in these
early poems. Its power, and even its sense, can be destroyed
if the editor allows himself even a modified system of reliance
on the almost always unsystematic punctuation[1]; capitalization and spelling too must be systematized if they are not to
introduce incongruous and distracting effects which may
impede, if not destroy, meaning. Again the editor must con-
stantly be on the watch for English archaisms (distinguishing
significant from non-significant variations of spelling[2]), and
for, say, a Greek construction or some build-up of Latin
rhetoric, which can only be given shape in our less inflected
language by something like an eighteenth-century technique
of punctuation. Then, while rescuing Shelley's usually admir-
able periods from the anacolutha into which his manuscript
punctuation is liable to degrade them, the editor must play
fair with his reader by signifying where the poet has indeed
corrupted his own meaning, as he sometimes does, by miscopying or lack of revision.

Though to most people all this might well seem a gratuitous
assertion of things long known and demonstrated, there will
be not a few today to whom it might appear both new and
heretical to suggest that the editing of Shelley's manuscripts
involves more than their printed reproduction in accordance
with a few formulae. Such faith, alas, is simpler than the
reality. The path, if there is one, can be sought only by a

---

[1] Very frequently the whole effect of a long passage will hang on a compli-
cated piece of syntactical structure, the syntax on the punctuation and the
punctuation on the editor's own resourcefulness, that of the manuscript being
either inadequate or definitely misleading: e.g. No. 24. 31–52, and the last few
lines of No. 51. See also nn. on No. 50, where, as often, a modern editor has to
be grateful for the work of Dowden, Hutchinson, and his other accomplished
predecessors.

[2] For the strange rationalizing of H. Buxton Forman on this subject see
N. Rogers, 'Shelley's Spelling', in *Keats–Shelley Memorial Bulletin*, no. xvi,
ed. Dorothy Hewlett, 1965.

reasoned, point-by-point analysis not merely of one or two manuscripts but of many; nor can this be done without a constant study of Shelley's thought and linguistic equipment. As with the text of the so-called 'scholarly modern' editing, so with the accompanying apparatus: it is based not on principles of critical selection but upon a comprehensiveness which industriously seeks to cover all points and to treat all points alike. I hope that *The Esdaile Poems* has not suffered from the limitation of my textual apparatus to points which seemed to me to have significance. Similarly in my 'Notes to the Text' I have tried to resist, as far as I could, the attraction of 'source-hunting'—an attraction none the less great because dogged by the perils of *post hoc propter hoc* reasoning—and merely to notice, without multiplying examples, the general nature of the influences underlying these early poems. Not least interesting is the influence of Erasmus Darwin, to whose work Shelley was drawn through the influence of Dr. Lind. That Platonism, science, and the wilder rabidities of libertarian language should come to him from a single source is characteristic of the fusions that went to make up his Renaissance mind during his Eton period. Mr. Desmond King-Hele has most kindly permitted me a preview of his article on Erasmus Darwin, published in the *Keats–Shelley Memorial Bulletin*, no. xvi, and for this I am greatly indebted both to him and to Miss Dorothy Hewlett, editor of the *Bulletin*.

I have to record my deep gratitude to the late Mr. W. C. H. Esdaile who generously granted permission for the publication of this Oxford Text, and to Mr. James Lees-Milne, through whose kind offices this was arranged. My thanks are due to Messrs. Sotheby & Co. for allowing me a valuable last-minute examination of the Notebook before its sale, on 2 July, 1962[1];

---

[1] The manuscript of the present volume was in the hands of my publisher when the Carl H. Pforzheimer Library announced their purchase of the Note-book. Their printed version, published by Alfred Knopf in New York, and by Faber & Faber in London, is an outstanding example of the rapid, well-organized labour of Professor Kenneth Neill Cameron, its editor, and his staff. In addition to a text it contains much interesting and often significant information.

to Texas Christian University for a photostat of one of Shelley's letters; and to Mr. and Mrs. Donald H. Reiman for their energetic care in the checking of my text.

It would be impossible to name all those whose long encouragement and generous help underlie my work on Shelley's manuscripts: perhaps they will not think me ungrateful if the thanks I offer are collective. I must, however, offer commemorative gratitude to four whose wisdom and experience are, alas, no longer with us: Professor H. W. Garrod, Miss Helen Darbyshire, Mr. Percy Simpson, and Mr. J. B. Leishman. For my errors and opinions I am, of course, solely responsible, but if there be any good in this edition it owes something to their kindness. In my huge task of editing a complete text of Shelley's poetry the field of error is correspondingly huge and intimidating. But I hope that my trial of methods in this preliminary volume may result in the improvement of my main volumes which will follow.

NEVILLE ROGERS

Ohio University
Athens, Ohio, U.S.A.

CONTENTS

APPENDIX: POEMS NOT BY SHELLEY OR OF DOUBTFUL
AUTHORSHIP

By Elizabeth Shelley

Probably by Harriet Shelley

LIST OF PLATES

SIGNS USED
AND BOOKS REFERRED TO

MANUSCRIPTS

BM   British Museum

Esd.   Esdaile Notebook

NYPL   Berg Collection, New York Public Library

Pf.   Pforzheimer Library, New York

TCU   W. L. Lewis Collection, Texas Christian University

PRINTED EDITIONS

Shelley, *Queen Mab*. Privately printed, 1813.

Shelley, *Alastor; or, The Spirit of Solitude*. Baldwin, Cradock & Joy, 1816.

The Poetical Works of Shelley, ed. Mrs. Shelley. Moxon, 1839.

Thomas Medwin, *Life of Shelley* [ed. H. Buxton Forman. Oxford, 1913], 1847.

T. J. Hogg, *Life of Shelley* [ed. Humbert Wolfe. Dent, 1933], 1858.

The Poetical Works of Shelley, ed. W. M. Rossetti. Moxon, 1870.

Edward Dowden, *Life of Shelley*. Kegan Paul, 1886.

Shelley, *The Wandering Jew*, ed. Bertram Dobell. Reeves & Turner, 1887

The Poetical Works of Shelley, ed. Thomas Hutchinson. Oxford, 1904

A. Koszul, *La Jeunesse de Shelley*. Bloud, Paris, 1910.

The Poetical Works of Shelley, ed. C. D. Locock. Methuen, 1911.

H. Buxton Forman, *The Shelley Notebooks*. Privately printed for the Boston Bibliophile Society, St. Louis, Mo., 1911.

MISCELLANEOUS

Robert Bridges, *The Spirit of Man*. Longmans, Green, 1916.

R. B. McKerrow, *An Introduction to Bibliography for Literary Students*, 2nd impression. Oxford, 1928.

Newman Ivey White, *Shelley*. Secker & Warburg, 1947.

Kenneth Neill Cameron, *The Young Shelley*. Gollancz, 1951.

J. A. Notopoulos, *The Platonism of Shelley*. Duke University Press, Durham, N.C., 1949.

Neville Rogers, *Shelley at Work*. Oxford, 1956.

Fredson Bowers, *Textual and Literary Criticism*. C.U.P., 1959

Kenneth Neill Cameron, *Shelley and His Circle*, Vols. I and II. Oxford, 1960.

Frederick L. Jones, *The Letters of Shelley*, 2 vols. Oxford, 1964.

The *Oxford English Dictionary*.

⟨ ⟩ denotes letters or words supplied conjecturally or textually doubtful.[1]

[ ] in the Textual Commentary denotes words or letters cancelled in the manuscript.

[ ] in titles and elsewhere denotes words or letters implicit in the manuscript and supplied for clarity.

[1] See Introd., § 1, p. xxiv, below.

HISTORY OF
SHELLEY'S EARLY MINOR POEMS
AND THEIR MANUSCRIPTS

WHAT Shelley thought about his early minor poems is plain from passages in letters to Miss Hitchener written about the beginning of the year 1812. Since 'liberty' was their main theme they were 'not wholly useless'; nevertheless they were 'inferior productions . . . only valuable to philosophical and reflecting minds who love to trace the early state of human feelings and opinions . . .'.[1] He hoped that the libertarian theme might move men's minds a little, and that their sale among the rich might produce profits which he could devote to the poor; herein he was thinking, more especially, of helping the lot of the Irish. The poems mark the early stages in which the energetic prose-pamphleteer became merged in the poet. Thanks to the survival of the notebook into which they were transcribed 'the history of Shelley's imagination from the days at Oxford to the days at Tremadoc is no longer a blank'.[2]

One reason why Shelley's plans for his little volume were not fulfilled was that they were displaced by the writing of *Queen Mab*. They had been delayed, in the meanwhile, by the misadventures of the manuscript. R. and J. Stockdale, the Dublin printers to whom Shelley and Harriet consigned it in February 1812, would seem to have set up part of it in print, but by August they were refusing to continue the work until they were paid. The correspondence of the two Shelleys in 1812 bears witness to their concern with the recovery of the manuscript. The common assumption that they did, eventually, recover it has usually been bound up with a second assump-

---

[1] Frederick L. Jones, *The Letters of Percy Bysshe Shelley*, 2 vols., Clarendon Press, 1964, i. 214, 239.
[2] Edward Dowden, *The Life of Percy Bysshe Shelley*, 2 vols., Kegan Paul, 1886, i. 345.

tion, namely that the Stockdale manuscript is identical with the Esdaile Notebook. This Notebook, into which Shelley and Harriet transcribed the poems printed in the present volume, has always been so called because, until its sale at Sotheby's in May 1962, it was preserved at Cothelstone House, near Taunton, Somerset, by the Esdaile family, into which Ianthe Shelley, Harriet's daughter, was married after the death of her parents.

Until quite recently almost everything printed from or about the Esdaile Notebook derived from Dowden, who was allowed to examine it in the eighteen-eighties and to print selected lines. Dowden noticed that, if we exclude the two sonnets, dated 1813, and the five poems written in later by Harriet, the preceding fifty-one pieces correspond more or less to a line-count which he made in the manuscript,[1] and that this line-count corresponds roughly with an estimate concerning his 'other poems' made in a letter to Hookham.[2] This has usually been accepted as clinching the identification. Oddly enough neither Dowden nor anybody else seems to have noticed that among the Esdaile poems dated by Shelley are two (Nos. 25 and 32) composed in August 1812—within the very period when he and Harriet were trying to recover the Stockdale manuscript. Dowden[3] not only dated those poems but rightly observed that two other poems (Nos. 26 and 27) must, from their subject-matter, also belong to August 1812. Quite clearly, if there is a correspondence between the two manuscripts, it cannot be a complete one.

The possibility of a partial correspondence must be considered. It is not necessary to suppose that when Shelley wrote out the Esdaile poems he had the Stockdale manuscript with him. He could have made use of other documents, of memory, or of both. Some have supposed that he received the papers from Stockdale at Tremadoc in the winter of 1812–13.

---

[1] Dowden, *Life*, i. 345. Cf. commentary on No. 51, p. 108 below.
[2] Jones, *Letters of Shelley*, i. 350.
[3] Dowden, *Life*, i. 283–4, 293–5, 404.

Good arguments against this have been advanced by Professor Kenneth Neill Cameron,[1] who suggests instead that he may have recovered it on his second expedition to Dublin, in 1813. Failing definite evidence, however, one might doubt whether the alarms and discursions of that period would have allowed the necessary time or mood.[2] We shall be safe in regarding the recovery of the Stockdale Manuscript as 'not proven' and the Esdaile Notebook as being, in any case, the somewhat divergent record of his early, minor poems with which Shelley intended to replace it.

[1] Kenneth Neill Cameron, *The Young Shelley*, Gollancz, 1951, 381–2.
[2] For the biographical background see Newman Ivey White, *Shelley*, Secker & Warburg, 1947, vol. i, ch. x; or Dowden, *Life*, vol. i, ch. vii.

INTRODUCTION

THE purpose of this volume is to present a text of the poems in the Esdaile Notebook, collated with other relevant manuscripts and printed sources.

§ 1. *The Esdaile Notebook*

The Notebook measures 181 mm. × 114 mm. It is bound in marble boards with original red half-roan and contains 88 pages of writing followed by pages left blank. The poems number 58. Nos. 1–53 are in Shelley's handwriting, Nos. 54–58 in the hand of Harriet, his first wife. That the Notebook was intended as a gift to Harriet is suggested by the insertion of the first poem before the original heading, 'Poems', and the addition of the two sonnets, Nos. 52 and 53, after Shelley's final line-count. All the contents have the character of intermediate fair copies, written out for the preservation of the poems rather than for the use of the printer. The penmanship is mainly good and often beautiful, though it sometimes lapses through fatigue. Doubtful readings and passages where meaning has been distorted by probable miscopying have been indicated in the text.[1]

§ 2. *Authorship*

Of the 53 poems written out by Shelley 51 are his own. The other two, Nos. 43[2] and 45,[3] are by his sister Elizabeth. Of the 5 in Harriet Shelley's handwriting No. 54 must, surely, be

---

[1] See p. xviii, 'Signs Used'.

[2] So Shelley informed Hogg. See Jones, *Letters of Shelley*, i. 43. I am accepting Shelley's statement, though it is not impossible that he made it to impress Hogg. Some form of joint authorship is also possible.

[3] T. J. Hogg, *The Life of Shelley*, ed. Humbert Wolfe, Dent, 1933, i. 126.

taken, as Dowden[1] took it, to be by Shelley. Nor need we doubt that Nos. 56 and 58, though crude and immature, are authentically his. Nos. 55 and 57 are on an altogether lower level of accomplishment and seem, more likely than anything else, to be pathetic effusions by Harriet herself.

Nos. 43, 45, 55, and 57 have here been printed in an Appendix.

§ 3. *Other Manuscripts*

For 11 out of the 58 poems in the Esdaile Notebook other manuscripts can be identified. One, a manuscript of No. 33,[2] seems to have disappeared. The remainder are now distributed between the British Museum, the New York Public Library, the Pforzheimer Library, and Texas Christian University. The location of each, together with conflicts of dating and divergences in form, is best shown by tabular comparison:

Esd.	Date	Other MSS.	Date	Divergence
14	1811	BM, letter to E. Hitchener	7 Jan. 1812	Shorter by 5 stanzas, 4 lines
17		BM, letter to E. Hitchener	14 Feb. 1812	orter by 1 stanza
19	1810[3]	Pf., loose sheet given to Hogg		Shorter by 20 lines
[33	1810	loose sheets[2] given to Hogg		Stanzas 1 and 3 each shorter by 2 lines]
35	1810	Pf., letter to Hogg	19 June 1811	3rd stanza replaced by variant stanza from Esd. 34.
36	3 Sept. 1809	Pf., letter to Hogg	17 May 1811	
41	1810	TCU, letter to Hogg	28 Apr. 1811	
43		Pf., letter to Hogg	11 Jan. 1811	1 stanza more than the 3 stanzas of Esd.

---

[1] Dowden, *Life*, i. 413.

[2] This manuscript was given by Hogg in 1834 to the Norfolk antiquary, Dawson Turner, and is presumed to have been sold at the sale of his effects in 1859, after which its whereabouts ceased to be known. See *Shelley and His Circle*, ii. 644.

[3] 'Written at Oxford', Hogg, *Life*, i, 124.

Esd.	Date	Other MSS.	Date	Divergence
44	1809	Pf., letter to Hogg	6 Jan. 1811	2 stanzas more than the 3 stanzas of Esd.
45	1808	Pf., loose sheets given to Hogg		5 stanzas, 14 lines more than the 3 stanzas of Esd.
47		NYPL, letter to E. F. Graham	c. 19 June 1811	1 stanza only against Esd. 6 stanzas plus refrain

We may look in vain among the divergences of these manuscripts for indications of a 'superior' text. The letter dates
are unreliable and possibly the Esdaile dates too. Nor can we
assume that a later date, even if provable, is evidence of
Shelley's considered revision. Changes in a later manuscript
may be due, no less probably, to miscopying, spontaneous
adaptation, or the vagaries of memory.[1]

My text, except where I have preferred Shelley's own printed
authority, has been that of the Esdaile Notebook. Other
manuscripts have been collated.

§ 4. *Printed Authority*

Shelley printed versions of 4 of the Esdaile poems—Nos. 1,
6, 21, and 45—and $11\frac{1}{2}$ lines from a fifth, No. 24. Textually the
later version of No. 1, printed as the Dedication with *Queen
Mab*, must claim preference. I have, however, printed both
versions in my text and hope that, in giving priority of place
to the Esdaile one, I have respected both Shelley's intentions
and the just claims of Harriet. For No. 6 I have used Shelley's
text of 1813, printed among the Notes to *Queen Mab*, and for
No. 21 the considerably revised version he printed in the
Alastor volume in 1816. His text of the lines from No. 24,
printed among the Notes to *Queen Mab*, are collated in my
Commentary.

[1] See 'Dating', p. xxxi below.

§ 5. *Accidentals*

In the matter of accidentals Shelley's manuscripts are an unsafe guide to his meaning. He always allowed room for the making of considerable adjustments on the printed page.

For most of his life he was accustomed, like Keats, Clare, and others, to leave much of his spelling, capitalization, and punctuation to be regularized by somebody else, if necessary by his publisher or printer. This was a tradition which dated back to the sixteenth century.[1]

In his later years Shelley became much concerned about errors. It seems likely that he quite under-estimated his own responsibility for much of the printer's difficulty.

Times there are when Shelley's spelling contains an archaism intended for especial effect, but these are not very common. Reasoning from an insufficient number of instances H. Buxton Forman[2] endeavoured to discover nuance, and even grammatical significance, in *desart*, *tyger*, and other such forms. A wider examination of instances will show that they are due simply to Shelley's indifference or haste. To preserve them is to introduce an artificial quaintness which he did not intend. Nothing is added to our knowledge of the poet by printing or annotating such everyday misspellings as *mein* for *mien*, *thier* for *their*, *hugh* for *huge*, *it's* for *its*, &c., nor such abbreviations as *thro*, *cd*, *wd*, *shd*, &c. All these have been silently regularized. So has the use of the hyphen, the possessive apostrophe, and the ampersand. Doubtful instances are noted in the commentary. Certain forms I have left, as Shelley does, to take care of themselves, e.g. past participles and past tenses such as *stamped/stampt*, *caressed/carest*, &c., *O* and *oh* (though, like

---

[1] The contrary is now sometimes asserted. But see R. B. McKerrow, *An Introduction to Bibliography for Literary Students*, Clarendon Press, 2nd impression, 1928, pp. 246–7, 250 ; and Fredson Bowers, *Textual and Literary Criticism*, C.U.P., 1959, pp. 126, 136.

[2] *The Shelley Notebooks*, privately printed for the Boston Bibliophile Society, St. Louis, Mo., 1911. See note on 41. 10. See N. Rogers, 'Shelley's Spelling', in *Keats–Shelley Memorial Bulletin*, no. xvi, ed. Dorothy Hewlett, 1965.

Shelley, I prefer the first for a vocative), and *aye/ay* (though, again like Shelley, I prefer the first).

Capital letters too I have treated in the nineteenth-century fashion, that is to say that I have regularized them throughout, in accordance with the context. Some writers, e.g. Blake, Carlyle, Fitzgerald, did indeed use them for special effect upon the printed page. But in Shelley's manuscripts, as in much educated handwriting, even within the present century, they were often little more than a calligraphic ornament. To preserve them is, once again, to obtrude an artificial, distracting quaintness,[1] and sometimes something worse.[2]

In the matter of punctuation Shelley's fair copies range between the unhelpful and the misleading.[3] As No. 5 appears in the Notebook its two ten-line stanzas are unpunctuated except for a dash before the vocative in line 10 and an exclamation mark at the end of that line. Here, luckily, the syntax is so simple that the meaning is hardly impaired. Less simple is the opening stanza of No. 20, where a fifteen-line sentence, having its main verb in the thirteenth line, is unpunctuated save for a final exclamation mark. Sometimes he

[1] e.g. the not unpleasing Orientalism suggested by such manuscript capitalization as 'Month of Love' [8. 19], 'Sons of the Wind' [41. 1], 'Sister of Snow' [44. 19]. Since such examples have no significance I have not encumbered my footnotes with them.

[2] e.g. the apparently vocative adverb 'O Ever' [5. 11] or the untidy 'Its' in the middle of a line and sentence [27. 12]. Few eyes, one would imagine, could so combine pedantry and insensitiveness as to remain unoffended by these. For examples of sensitive editorial understanding cf. Hutchinson's fine capitals in 27. 8 and 50. 121.

[3] A *locus classicus* for editors of Shelley might be found in Robert Bridges's experience with the Platonic syntax of *Prometheus Unbound*, iii. 3. 44 foll., of which he wrote [*The Spirit of Man*, n. on No. 68], 'The great beauty of this passage suffers from the involved grammar, which deepens its obscurities, while the original punctuation still further hampers it. I have entirely discarded Shelley's punctuation, and added some capitals, hoping to make a more readable text.' His reference is here to the printed *textus receptus*. Writing to W. B. Yeats of the Bodleian MS. he notes that it is, in the matter of punctuation, &c. 'almost worse than nothing' [See N. Rogers, *Shelley at Work*, Clarendon Press, 1956, p. 135 n.] Few, at any time, can have been endowed with more of the necessary judgement and expertise than the late Laureate. Yet in a later edition of his anthology he was glad to print an improvement or two suggested by Henry Bradley.

The Bodleian MS. in question is a well-penned intermediate fair copy.

does afford a little help. The opening of No. 9 is an instance:

> In that strange mental wandering when to live
> To breathe, to be, is undivided joy
> When the most woe worn wretch wd. cease to grieve
> When satiation's self would fail to cloy;
> When unpercipient of all other things
> Than those that press around, the breathing Earth
> The gleaming sky & the fresh seasons birth,
> Sensation all it[s] wondrous rapture brings
> And to itself not once the mind recurs
> Is it foretaste of Heaven?

As an indication that the words between them form a complete sense-unit the commas in lines 6 and 7 have some value. But they are not enough: what we need is a parenthesis, strongly marked. And though the semicolon in line 4 does serve to group the first four 'when'-clauses together we need something in line 9 which would balance it and group together the remaining clauses before we reach the main verb. Shelley's punctuation of manuscripts, in short, is seldom adequate, even where it does happen to afford some help, and may never be safely trusted. Examples here are restricted to passages where sentence construction is affected. It is here, in his long, Latinate periods, that his meaning is most seriously involved.[1] As a rule his syntax is clear and skilful, and none the less so for its elaboration.

Two special idiosyncrasies need mention. One is his addiction to the dotted suspension point. This stop, usually of three dots, but occasionally of more or less than three, is for him an all-purpose affair which varies in significance. Literally introduced into a modern text it would mislead the reader by seeming to represent an ellipsis, probably intended for a dramatic aposiopesis. I have found, as Professor Jones does,[2] that more often than not it merely signifies the end of a sentence and requires replacement by a full stop, exclamation

---

[1] For an outstanding example cf. 46. 103–20 where preservation of the nonsensical manuscript semicolons in lines 104, 107, and 116 would reduce the whole long passage to an anacoluthon.

[2] *Letters of Shelley*, p. vii.

mark, or interrogation mark. In his own printings Shelley frequently so replaced it: e.g. the 1813 printing of 6. 32. In 6. 29, however, a dramatic aposiopesis does seem wanted, and here and in a few other places I follow his use of dots.

Another common anomaly, equally due to speed of writing, is what may be called 'anticipatory' stopping. Thus in 39. 36–37 Shelley writes

> Sweet flower! that blooms amid the weeds
> Where the rank serpent interest feeds

although the exclamatory force governs that whole sentence, so that the strong stop needs to be placed at its end.

> Sweet flower, that blooms amid the weeds
> Where the rank serpent Interest feeds!

Sometimes, as here, the anticipatory exclamation mark might be thought to represent no more than the once-fashionable way of pointing a vocative. That, however, will not explain such instances as 40. 23–24:

> O this were joy! & such as none would fear
> To purchase by a life of passing woe

where, again, the exclamation mark of the manuscript needs to be transferred to the end of the sentence. At times the effect of this tendency is quite irrational, as when the manuscript of 10.23 reads

> True! Mountain Liberty alone can heal. . . .

which could only make sense if he meant 'It is true that . . .'. Once again Shelley's mind, being too far ahead of his pen, has anticipated an exclamatory force in the sentence by attaching his stop to an early word in it.

Though Shelley's printings must, of course, be preferred as a rule, there are places when they cannot be regarded as the final indication of his intentions. Thus in No. 6, line 74, I have followed the manuscript italicization

Whilst the snakes whose smile *even him* defiled

in preference to the 1813 version 'even him *defiled*', whereby the irony is diminished.[1] Again in lines 47 and 64 of this poem I have ventured to omit some unhelpful commas which had crept in in 1813. These few deviations from my copy-text are noted in the Commentary.

In the whole matter of accidentals I have endeavoured to consider meaning rather than to aim at consistency or to systematize details. That this was Shelley's own principle may be shown by an examination of the text of the Pisa *Adonais* of 1821, about which he took particular pains. In punctuation my concern, like his, has been largely with syntax.[2] Like previous editors I have adjusted non-significant minutiae without attempting to systematize.[3]

§ 6. *Headings and Titles*

Of the fifty-three poems transcribed by Shelley in the Note-book, forty-four are printed here with the titles that appear in his manuscript; one of these, that of No. 4, he left incomplete, but the name of the plant he had forgotten is unimportant. For No. 1 I have printed the title added by Harriet to Shelley's transcription, and for Nos. 54, 56, and 58 the titles which head her own transcriptions. For No. 34 I have used the simple and obvious title printed by Rossetti in 1870. 'Bigotry's Victim', Hogg's time-honoured title for No. 41, was a euphemism adapted to his doctored text: since, however, it is faithful to the poem as a whole and to Shelley's Lucretian use of the word 'Religion' I have preserved it. Five poems

---

[1] Though C. D. Locock, in *Poetical Works*, 1911, takes the opposite view.

[2] For Shelley's own unconcern about system for its own sake, cf. *Adonais* 2, 'O, weep for Adonais!' with lines 19 and 72 where he has 'Oh weep for Adonais!'; again line 306 has 'oh! that it should be so!', while in 476 he prints 'oh, hasten thither'.

[3] Thus, in *The Complete Poetical Works of Percy Bysshe Shelley*, Oxford, 1904, reprinted 1956, pp. 432, 433, Thomas Hutchinson adds commas after the 'Oh' in *Adonais* 19 and 72, but does not attempt to regularize the other details.

which lack manuscript headings—Nos. 20, 22, 35, 45, 55, 57—
have been headed by quotation of the opening line. My com-
prehensive title for Nos. 37–40 does not appear in the manuscript. Apart from this I have resorted to invention only twice:
with No. 21, where neither the opening line nor Mary Shelley's
title in 1839 would catch the Platonic purport significant in
Shelley's development; and with No. 42, where I hope that
the title I have ventured is both inoffensively descriptive and
more apt than a heading from the first line.

§ 7. *Dating*

If we may trust Harriet Shelley's dating for Nos. 58 and 54
the period of Shelley's composition covered by the Esdaile
poems ranges from 28 February 1805[1] to May 1814. For
present purposes the dates given in the manuscript must, in
the main, be accepted, but as we do not know how far they
came from reliable documents and how far from memory
they cannot be regarded as final. Sometimes a date in the
Notebook is in conflict with the date of a letter wherein Shelley
transcribed the poem, or some version of it. But the letter dates
too are unreliable guides, since even where Shelley is pre-
senting a poem to a friend as a new one it may have been merely
something he had rummaged up from papers or memory.[2]

The dating of poems in my text falls into five approximate
categories:

(i) twenty-five poems dated from the manuscript, namely
Nos. 14, 15, 16, 18, 25, 32, 33, 34, 35, 36, 37, 38, 39, 40, 41, 42,
44, 45, 46, 50, 52, 53, 54, 55, 58.

(ii) Two poems dated from Shelley's correspondence: Nos. 17
and 47.

---

[1] Dowden [*Life*, i. 48] seems unduly sceptical about this date.

[2] E.g. No. 41, for which I have accepted the *Esd.* dating, 1810, is described
in the letter to Hogg of April 28, 1811, as 'a mad effusion of this morning'.
For Shelley's reliance on memory see Hogg, *Life*, i. 126. An example
of its vagaries was his quotation in a letter of two stanzas of No. 35, supple-
mented by a stanza from No. 34 in place of the third stanza which he could
not remember. See Cameron, *Shelley and His Circle*, ii. 809–12.

(iii) Five poems arising out of Shelley's devotion to his wife Harriet which may be ascribed to 1811–12: Nos. 1, 5, 8, 24, 29.

(iv) Twenty-four poems datable, with varying degrees of certainty, from biographical, internal, or other evidence: Nos. 2, 3, 4, 6, 7, 9, 10, 11, 12, 13, 19, 20, 21, 22, 23, 26, 27, 28, 30, 31, 43, 48, 49, 51.

(v) Two poems which cannot be dated: No. 57, of which the authorship is uncertain, and No. 56 where the manuscript date is improbable and other evidence is lacking.

Points arising from this dating are referred to in the Textual Commentary and in the Notes.

§ 8. *Collation*

Since this volume has been planned as part of my complete Oxford Edition of Shelley's poetry I have preferred to the versions in the Esdaile Notebook such printings of his as may claim to represent his *ultima manus*; see § 4, above. Since the many other edited versions are not witnesses to the text they are not noticed in my footnotes, apart from a few widely reproduced readings which need correction. A word is called for about the 'corrections' made by the editors of the Julian Edition from 'a careful transcript' of the Esdaile Notebook. Reduplicated quotation has invested these with undue value. Use of the transcript was limited to poems and passages which, in 1927–9, had already been published, and the advantage taken of it was less than it might have been; accuracy apart, the editors do not seem to have understood, for instance, that the correction of one version of a poem from another version, when there are differences in the arrangement and number of the lines and stanzas, can produce no more than a bewildering conflation. Though he must often differ from them a modern editor owes much to Dowden, Rossetti, Hutchinson, and even Hogg, if only for their valuable help with the problem of pointing, bequeathed by Shelley.

Since the poems in the Appendix do not belong to Shelley's

text collation has been restricted to the printing of certain stanzas of which there are manuscripts outside the Esdaile Notebook.

Among the editions referred to I do not include the non-Esdaile versions of Nos. 19, 35, 36, 43, 44, and 45, published by Professor Kenneth Neill Cameron in *Shelley and His Circle*. These are not texts but printed transcriptions of manuscripts, and I have gratefully made use of their witness as such. For non-Esdaile texts outside the Pforzheimer collection I have been permitted to examine the originals or to obtain photocopies.

THE ESDAILE POEMS

1

TO HARRIET [SHELLEY]

1811–12

VERSION I

Whose is the love that, gleaming through the world,
Wards off the poisonous arrow of its scorn?
    Whose is the warm and partial praise,
    Virtue's most sweet reward?

Whose looks gave grace to the majestic theme,   5
The sacred, free and fearless theme of truth?
    Whose form did I gaze fondly on,
    And love mankind the more?

Harriet! on thine:—thou wert my purer soul;
Thou wert the inspiration to my song;   10
    Thine are these early wilding flowers,
    Though garlanded by me.

Then twine the withering wreath-buds round thy brow:
Its bloom may deck their pale and faded prime,—
    Can they survive without thy love   15
    Their wild and moody birth?

TITLE: *Esd., in Harriet Shelley's handwriting. See n.* AUTOGRAPH: *Version I:*
Esd. PRINTED: *Version II: Shelley, with* Queen Mab, *1813.* TEXT: *Version I:*
Esd. Version II: 1813. DATE: *See Intr. § 7.*

VERSION II

Whose is the love that, gleaming through the world,
Wards off the poisonous arrow of its scorn?
   Whose is the warm and partial praise,
   Virtue's most sweet reward?

Beneath whose looks did my reviving soul   5
Riper in truth and virtuous daring grow?
   Whose eyes have I gazed fondly on,
   And loved mankind the more?

Harriet! on thine:—thou wert my purer mind;
Thou wert the inspiration of my song;   10
   Thine are these early wilding flowers,
   Though garlanded by me.

Then press unto thy breast this pledge of love,
And know, though time may change and years may roll,
   Each flowret gathered in my heart   15
   It consecrates to thine.

2

A SABBATH WALK

Probably late 1811 or early 1812

Sweet are the stilly forest glades:
Imbued with holiest feelings there
I love to linger pensively
   And court seclusion's smile;
This mountain labyrinth of loveliness   5
Is sweet to me even when the frost has torn

TITLE, AUTOGRAPH, TEXT: *Esd.* DATE: *See n. The title is preceded by the word
'Poems', which suggests that No. 1 was a later addition.*

All save the ivy clinging to the rocks
Like friendship to a friend's adversity!
   Yes! in my soul's devotedness
   I love to linger in the wilds: 10
   I have my God and worship him,
   O vulgar souls, more ardently
      Than ye the Almighty fiend
      Before whose throne ye kneel.

'Tis not the soul pervading all,   15
'Tis not the fabled cause that framed
The everlasting orbs of Heaven
   And this eternal earth,
Nor the cold Christians' bloodstained King of Kings
Whose shrine is in the temple of my heart,—   20
'Tis that Divinity whose work and self
Is harmony and wisdom, truth and love;
   Who, in the forests' rayless depth,
   And in the cities' wearying glare,
   In sorrow, solitude and death,   25
      Accompanies the soul
      Of him who dares be free.

It is a lovely winter's day;
Its brightness speaks of Deity,
Such as the good man venerates,   30
   Such as the Poet loves;
Ah! softly o'er the quiet of the scene
A pealing harmony is felt to rise.—
The village bells are sweet, but they denote
That spirits love by the clock, and are devout   35
   All at a stated hour; the sound
   Is sweet to sense, but to the heart
   It tells of worship insincere,
      Creeds half-believed,—the ear that bends

19 Christians'] Christians *Esd.*   23 forests'] forests *Esd.*

To custom, prejudice and fear,   40
The tongue that's bought to speak,
The heart that's hired to feel.

But to the man sincerely good
Each day will be a Sabbath day,
Consigned to thoughts of holiness,   45
    And deeds of living love:
The God he serves requires no cringing creed,
No idle prayers, no senseless mummeries,
No gold, no temples and no hireling priests,—
The winds, the pine-boughs and the waters make   50
    Its melody. The hearts of all
    The beings it pervadeth form
    A temple for its purity;—
The wills of those that love the right
    Are offerings beyond   55
    Thanksgivings, prayers and gold.

3

THE CRISIS

? 1810–11

When we see Despots prosper in their weakness,
When we see Falsehood triumph in its folly,
When we see Evil, Tyranny, Corruption,
    Grin, grow and fatten,—

When Virtue toileth through a world of sorrow,   5
When Freedom dwelleth in the deepest dungeon,
When Truth in chains and infamy bewaileth
    O'er a world's ruin,—

TITLE, AUTOGRAPH, TEXT: *Esd.*   DATE: *See n.*

When Monarchs laugh upon their thrones securely,
Mocking the woes which are to them a treasure, 10
Hear the deep curse, and quench the mother's hunger
    In her child's murder;—

Then may we hope the consummating hour
Dreadfully, sweetly, swiftly is arriving
When light from darkness, peace from desolation 15
    Bursts unresisted,—

Then, 'mid the gloom of doubt and fear and anguish,
The votaries of Virtue may raise their eyes to heaven,
And confident watch till the renovating day-star
    Gild the horizon. 20

4

PASSION

TO THE [   ]

? Early 1812

Fair are thy berries to the dazzled sight,
Fair is thy chequered stalk of mingling hues,
    And yet thou dost conceal
      A deadly poison there
        Uniting good and ill. 5

Art thou not like a lawyer whose smooth face
Doth promise good, while hiding so much ill?
    Ah, no! The semblance even
      Of goodness lingereth not
        Within that hollow eye. 10

AUTOGRAPH, TEXT: *Esd.* TITLE: *See n.* DATE: *See nn.*
7 Doth] Dost *Esd.*

Art thou the tyrant, whose unlovely brow
With rare and glittering gems is contrasted?
  No,—thou may'st kill the body:
    He withers up the soul,—
      Sweet thou when he is nigh!   15

Art thou the wretch whose cold and sensual soul
His hard-earned mite tears from the famished hind,
  Then says that God hath willed
    Many to toil and groan
      That few may boast at ease?   20

Art thou the slave whose mercenary sword,
Stained with an unoffending brother's blood,
  Deeper yet shows the spot
    Of cowardice, whilst he
      Who wears it talks of courage?   25

Ah, no! Else, while I gaze upon thy bane,
I should not feel unmingled with contempt
  This awful feeling rise:
    As if I stood at night
      In some weird ruin's shade.   30

Thou art like youthful passion's quenchless fire,
Which in some unsuspecting bosom glows:
  So wild, so beautiful,
    Possessing wondrous power
      To wither or to warm.   35

Essence of Virtue blasting Virtue's prime,
Bright bud of Truth producing Falsehood's fruit,
  Freedom's own soul, that binds
    The human will in chains
      Indissolubly fast,—   40

30 weird] wierd *above* [grey] in *Esd.*

Prime source of all that's lovely, good and great,
Debasing man below the meanest brute,
   Spring of all healing streams,
     Yet deadlier than the gall
       Blackening a monarch's heart,—   45

Why art thou thus, O Passion? Custom's chains
Have bound thee from thine heaven-directed flight,
   Or thou would'st never thus
     Bring misery to man,
       Uniting good and ill.   50

5

TO HARRIET [SHELLEY]

1811–12

Never, oh, never, shall yonder Sun
   Through my frame its warmth diffuse,
When the heart that beats in its faithful breast
   Is untrue, fair girl, to thee!—
     Nor the beaming moon   5
     On its nightly voyage
Shall visit this spirit with softness again,
     When its soaring hopes
     And its fluttering fears
Are untrue, fair girl, to thee!   10

Oh! ever, while this frail brain has life,
   Will it thrill to thy love-beaming gaze,
And whilst thine eyes with affection gleam,
   It will worship the spirit within,
     And when death comes   15
     To quench their fire,

TITLE, AUTOGRAPH, TEXT: *Esd.*   DATE: *See Intr.* § 7.

A sorrowful rapture their dimness will shed,
   As I bind me tight
   With thine auburn hair
And die, as I lived, with thee.   20

6

FALSEHOOD AND VICE

A DIALOGUE

? 1809–10

Whilst monarchs laughed upon their thrones
To hear a famished nation's groans,
And hugged the wealth wrung from the woe
That makes its eyes and veins o'erflow,—
Those thrones, high built upon the heaps   5
Of bones where frenzied Famine sleeps,
Where Slavery wields her scourge of iron,
Red with mankind's unheeded gore,
And War's mad fiends the scene environ,
Mingling with shrieks a drunken roar,—   10
There Vice and Falsehood took their stand,
High raised above the unhappy land.

FALSEHOOD

Brother! arise from the dainty fare,
Which thousands have toiled and bled to bestow;
A finer feast for thy hungry ear   15
Is the news that I bring of human woe.

AUTOGRAPH: *Esd.*   DATE: *See n.*   PRINTED: *Shelley, with* Queen Mab, *1813.*
TITLE, TEXT: *Shelley, 1813. Capitals, as in other edd., have been adjusted.*
   4 its *1813*] thier *Esd.*   7 wields *1813*] with *Esd.*   8 Red with *1813*]
Stained in *Esd.*   10 roar,—] roar, *1813* roar *Esd.*

VICE

And, secret one, what hast thou done,
To compare, in thy tumid pride, with me—
Me, whose career, through the blasted year,
Has been tracked by despair and agony? 20

FALSEHOOD

What have I done!—I have torn the robe
From baby Truth's unsheltered form,
And round the desolated globe
Borne safely the bewildering charm:
My tyrant-slaves to a dungeon-floor 25
Have bound the fearless innocent,
And streams of fertilizing gore
Flow from her bosom's hideous rent,
Which this unfailing dagger gave. . . .
I dread that blood!—No more!—this day 30
Is ours, though her eternal ray
    Must shine upon our grave.
Yet know, proud Vice, had I not given
To thee the robe I stole from Heaven,
Thy shape of ugliness and fear 35
Had never gained admission here.

VICE

And know, that had I disdained to toil,
But sate in my loathsome cave the while,
And ne'er to these hateful sons of Heaven,
GOLD, MONARCHY, and MURDER, given; 40
Hadst thou with all thine art essayed
One of thy games then to have played,
With all thine overweening boast,

---

18 me—] me? *1813* me *Esd.*   19 Me, whose] I whose *1813 and Esd.*
20 Has been tracked by despair and agony. *1813*] Has been marked by ruin
and misery *Esd.*   21 I have torn *1813*] I've torn *Esd.*   24 Borne *1813*]
Worn *Esd.*   26 fearless *1813*] dauntless *Esd.*   30 No more!] no more—
1813 no more. *Esd.*   32 grave. *1813*] grave . . . *Esd.*   34 robe *1813*]
mask *Esd.*   38 loathsome *1813*] noisome *Esd.*   40 and *1813*] or *Esd.*

Falsehood! I tell thee thou hadst lost!—
Yet wherefore this dispute?—we tend,   45
Fraternal, to one common end;
In this cold grave beneath my feet
Will our hopes, our fears, and our labours, meet.

FALSEHOOD

I brought my daughter, RELIGION, on earth:
She smothered Reason's babes in their birth;   50
But dreaded their mother's eye severe,—
So the crocodile slunk off slily in fear,
And loosed her bloodhounds from the den. . . .
They started from dreams of slaughtered men,
And, by the light of her poison eye,   55
Did her work o'er the wide earth frightfully:
The dreadful stench of her torches' flare,
Fed with human fat, polluted the air:
The curses, the shrieks, the ceaseless cries
Of the many-mingling miseries,   60
As on she trod, ascended high
And trumpeted my victory!—
Brother, tell what thou hast done.

VICE

I have extinguished the noon-day sun
In the carnage-smoke of battles won: 65
Famine, Murder, Hell and Power
Were glutted in that glorious hour
Which searchless Fate had stamped for me
With the seal of her security. . . .
For the bloated wretch on yonder throne   70
Commanded the bloody fray to rise.

---

44 hadst *1813*] had *Esd.*   45 Yet *1813*] But *Esd.*   47 feet *Esd.*]
feet, *1813*   50 Reason's babes *1813*] its sweetest buds *Esd.*   51 their
mother's *1813*] Reasons *Esd.*   57 dreadful *1813*] deathy *Esd.*   64 sun
Esd.] sun, *1813*   67 glutted *1813*] sated *Esd.*   glorious *1813*] joyous *Esd.*

Like me he joyed at the stifled moan
Wrung from a nation's miseries;
While the snakes, whose slime *even him* defiled,
In ecstasies of malice smiled: 75
They thought 'twas theirs,—but mine the deed!
Theirs is the toil, but mine the meed—
Ten thousand victims madly bleed.
They dream that tyrants goad them there
With poisonous war to taint the air: 80
These tyrants, on their beds of thorn,
Swell with the thoughts of murderous fame,
And with their gains to lift my name
Restless they plan from night to morn:
I—I do all; without my aid   85
Thy daughter, that relentless maid,
Could never o'er a death-bed urge
The fury of her venomed scourge.

FALSEHOOD

Brother, well:—the world is ours;
And whether thou or I have won,   90
The pestilence expectant lowers
On all beneath yon blasted sun.
Our joys, our toils, our honours meet
In the milk-white and wormy winding-sheet:
A short-lived hope, unceasing care,   95
Some heartless scraps of godly prayer,
A moody curse, and a frenzied sleep
Ere gapes the grave's unclosing deep,
A tyrant's dream, a coward's start,
The ice that clings to a priestly heart,   100

74 While *1813*] Whilst *Esd.*   *even him* defiled *Esd.*] even him *defiled 1813*;
see Intr. § *5.*   79 dream *1813*] think *Esd.*   80–81 *Esd. has*
                       [But hired assassins! tis not vice
                       Tis her sweet sister Cowardice . . .]
82 with the thoughts *1813*] in *above* [with] thier dreams *Esd.*   83 name
Esd.] name. *1813*

A judge's frown, a courtier's smile,
Make the great whole for which we toil;
And, brother, whether thou or I
Have done the work of misery,
It little boots: thy toil and pain,   105
Without my aid, were more than vain;
And but for thee I ne'er had sate
The guardian of Heaven's palace gate.

7

TO THE EMPERORS OF RUSSIA AND AUSTRIA WHO EYED THE BATTLE OF AUSTERLITZ FROM THE HEIGHTS WHILST BUONAPARTE WAS ACTIVE IN THE THICKEST OF THE FIGHT

? 1805–10

Coward Chiefs! who, while the fight
    Rages in the plain below,
Hide the shame of your affright
    On yon distant mountain's brow,—
Does one human feeling creep   5
Through your hearts' remorseless sleep?
On that silence cold and deep
    Does one impulse flow
Such as fires the Patriot's breast,
Such as breaks the Hero's rest?   10

No, cowards! Ye are calm and still—
    Keen frosts that blight the human bud,

TITLE, AUTOGRAPH, TEXT: *Esd.*   DATE: *See n.*

Each opening petal blight and kill,
   And bathe its tenderness in blood.
Ye hear the groans of those who die,   15
Ye hear the whistling death-shots fly
And, when the yells of victory
   Float o'er the murdered good,
Ye smile secure.—On yonder plain
The game, if lost, begins again.   20

Think ye the restless fiend who haunts
   The tumult of yon gory field,
Whom neither shame nor danger daunts,
   Who dares not fear, who cannot yield,
Will not with equalizing blow   25
Exalt the high, abase the low
And, in one mighty shock, o'erthrow
   The slaves that sceptres wield,—
Till from the ruin of the storm
Ariseth Freedom's awful form?   30

Hushed below the battle's jar
   Night rests silent on the heath,
Silent save when vultures soar
   Above the wounded warrior's death.
How sleep ye now, unfeeling Kings?   35
Peace seldom folds her snowy wings
On poisoned memory's conscience-stings
   Which lurk bad hearts beneath,
Nor downy beds procure repose
Where crime and terror mingle throes.   40

Yet may your terrors rest secure,—
   Thou, northern chief, why startest thou?
Pale Austria,—calm those fears! Be sure
   The tyrant needs such slaves as you!

33 when *possibly* where *Esd.*   34 warrior's] warriors *Esd.*

Think ye the world would bear his sway   45
Were dastards such as you away?
No! they would pluck his plumage gay,
   Torn from a nation's woe,
And lay him in the oblivious gloom
Where Freedom now prepares your tomb.   50

8

TO NOVEMBER

1811–12

O month of gloom, whose sullen brow
   Bears stamp of storms that lurk beneath,—
No care or horror bringest thou
   To one who draw his breath
Where Zephyrs play and sunbeams shine   5
Unstained by any fog of thine!

Whilst thou obscure'st the face of day
   Her radiant eyes can gild the gloom,
Darting a soft and vernal ray
   On Nature's leafless tomb,—   10
Yes, though the landscape's beauties flee,
My Harriet makes it spring to me!

Then raise thy fogs, invoke thy storms;
   Thy malice still my soul shall mar,
And, whilst thy rage the Heaven deforms,   15
   Shall laugh at every care;
And each pure feeling shall combine
To tell its Harriet 'I am thine!'

TITLE, AUTOGRAPH, TEXT: *Esd.*   DATE: *See Intr.* § 7.
  There is a cross against the title. Perhaps Shelley intended a footnote.
15 thy] the *Esd.*

It once was May; the month of love
    Did all it could to yield me pleasure,   20
Waking each green and vocal grove
    To a many-mingling measure;
But warmth and peace could not impart
To such a cold and shuddering heart.

Now thou art here—come, do thy worst   25
    To chill the breast that Harriet warms!
I fear me, sullen month, thou'lt burst
    With envy of her charms
And, finding nothing 's to be done,
Turn to December ere thou'st won!   30

9

WRITTEN ON A BEAUTIFUL DAY IN SPRING

? Spring 1812

In that strange mental wandering when to live,
    To breathe, to be, is undivided joy,
When the most woe-worn wretch would cease to grieve,
    When Satiation's self would fail to cloy;
When, unpercipient of all other things   5
    Than those that press around—the breathing Earth,
    The gleaming sky and the fresh season's birth—
Sensation all its wondrous rapture brings,
    And to itself not once the mind recurs;—
        Is it foretaste of Heaven?   10
    So sweet as this the nerves it stirs
And, mingling in the vital tide
    With gentle motion driven,

∧ 28 of *over* at *apparently, but possibly* at *over* of
∨ TITLE, AUTOGRAPH, TEXT: *Esd.*   DATE: *See nn.*
1–10 *For punctuation see Intr.* § *5.*

Cheers the sunk spirits, lifts the languid eye
And, scattering through the frame its influence wide,   15
Revives the spirits when they droop and die,
The frozen blood with genial beaming warms,
And to a gorgeous fly the sluggish worm transforms.

10

ON LEAVING LONDON FOR WALES
Autumn 1812

Thou miserable city!—where the gloom
Of penury mingles with the tyrant's pride,
And virtue bends in sorrow o'er the tomb
Where Freedom's hope and Truth's high courage died!
May floods and vales and mountains me divide   5
From all the taints thy wretched walls contain!—
That life's extremes, in desolation wide,
No more heap horrors on my beating brain
Nor sting my shuddering heart to sympathy with pain!

With joy I breathe the last and full farewell   10
That long has quivered on my burdened heart;
My natural sympathies to rapture swell
As from its day thy cheerless glooms depart;
Nor all the glare thy gayest scenes impart
Could lure one sigh, could steal one tear from me,   15
Or lull to languishment the wakeful smart
Which virtue feels for all 'tis forced to see,
Or quench the eternal flame of generous Liberty.

TITLE, AUTOGRAPH, TEXT: *Esd.*   DATE: *See n.*   PRINTED: *19–45, 55–63,*
Dowden, Life, 1886.
   2 tyrant's] tyrants *Esd.*   10 full *possibly* free *Esd.*

Hail to thee, Cambria, for the unfettered wind
    Which from thy wilds even now methinks I feel,   20
Chasing the clouds that roll in wrath behind,
    And tightening the soul's laxest nerves to steel!—
    True mountain Liberty alone may heal
The pain which Custom's obduracies bring!—
    And he who dares in fancy even to steal   25
One draught from Snowdon's ever sacred spring
Blots out the unholiest rede of wordly witnessing!

And shall that soul, to selfish peace resigned,
    So soon forget the woe its fellows share?
Can Snowdon's Lethe from the free-born mind   30
    So soon the page of injured penury tear?
    Does this fine mass of human passion dare
To sleep, unhonouring the patriot's fall,
    Or life's sweet load in quietude to bear
While millions famish even in Luxury's hall,   35
And Tyranny, high raised, stern lowers over all?

No, Cambria, never may thy matchless vales
    A heart so false to hope and virtue shield!—
Nor ever may thy spirit-breathing gales
    Waft freshness to the slaves who dare to yield!   40
    For me . . . the weapon that I burn to wield
I seek amid thy rocks to ruin hurled—
    That Reason's flag may over Freedom's field,
Symbol of bloodless victory, wave unfurled,
A meteor-sign of love effulgent o'er the world!   45

Hark to that shriek! My hand had almost clasped
    The dagger that my heart had cast away,
When the pert slaves whose wanton power had grasped
    All hope that springs beneath the eye of day,
    Pass before Memory's gaze in long array.   50

36 lowers *possibly* towers *Esd.*   over *Esd.*] on *1886*

The storm fleets by and calmer thoughts succeed,
  Feelings once more mild Reason's voice obey:
Woe be the tyrant's and the murderer's meed,—
But Nature's wound alone should make their conscience bleed.

Do thou, wild Cambria, calm each struggling thought;   55
  Cast thy sweet veil of rocks and woods between,
That by the soul to indignation wrought
  Mountains and dells be mingled with the scene;
  Let me forever be what I have been,
But not forever at my needy door   60
  Let Misery linger, speechless, pale and lean;
I am the friend of the unfriended poor,—
Let me not madly stain their righteous cause in gore.

No more! The visions fade before my sight
  Which Fancy pictures in the waste of air,   65
Like lovely dreams ere morning's chilling light;
  And sad realities alone are there.
  Ah! neither woe nor fear nor pain can tear
Their image from the tablet of my soul
  Nor the mad floods of despotism, where   70
Lashed into desperate furiousness they roll,
Nor Passion's soothing voice, not Interest's cold control.

11

A WINTER'S DAY

Probably 1811–12

O wintry day, that mockest Spring
  With hopes of the reviving year,

V **53** tyrant's . . . murderer's] tyrants . . . murderers *Esd.*
Λ TITLE, AUTOGRAPH, TEXT: *Esd.*   DATE: *See n.*

That sheddest softness from thy wing
And, near the cascades murmuring,
   Awakenest sounds so clear   5
That peals of vernal music swing
   Through the balm atmosphere!—

Why hast thou given, O year, to May
   A birth so premature,—
To live one uncompleted day?   10
That the mad whirlwind's sullen sway
   May sweep it from the moor,
And winter reassume the sway
   That shall so long endure?

Art thou like Genius' matin-bloom,—   15
   Unwelcome promise of its prime,
That scattereth its rich perfume
Around the portals of the tomb,
   Decking the scar of Time
In mockery of the early doom?   20

Art thou like Passion's rapturous dream,
   That o'er life's stormy dawn
Doth dart its wild and flamy beam,
Yet like a fleeting flash doth seem
   When many chequered years are gone,   25
⟨And tell the illusion of its gleam
   Life's blasted springs alone⟩?

Whate'er thou emblemest, I'll breathe
   Thy transitory sweetness now,
And whether Health with roseate wreath   30
May bind mine head, or creeping Death
   Steal o'er my pulse's flow,
Struggling the wintry winds beneath
   I'll love thy vernal glow.

4 cascades *thus Esd., but possibly for* cascade's   10 uncompleted]
incompleted *Esd.*   11 whirlwind's] whirlwinds *Esd.*   15 Genius'] Genius's
Esd.   26–27 *See n.*   32 pulse's] pulses *Esd.*

12

TO LIBERTY

? 1811–12

Oh, let not Liberty
  Silently perish!—
May the groan and the sigh
  Yet the flame cherish!
Till the voice to Nature's bursting heart given,   5
  Ascending loud and high,
  A world's indignant cry
  And, startling on his throne
  The tyrant grim and lone,
Shall beat the deaf vault of Heaven.   10

Say, can the Tyrant's frown
  Daunt those who fear not?
Or break the spirits down
  His badge that wear not?
Can chains or death or infamy subdue   15
  The free and fearless soul
  That dreads not their control,
  Sees Paradise and Hell,
  Sees the palace and the cell,
Yet bravely dares prefer the good and true?   20

Regal pomp and pride
  The Patriot falls in scorning:
The spot whereon he died
  Should be the despot's warning,—

TITLE, AUTOGRAPH, TEXT: *Esd.*   DATE: *See n.*   PRINTED: *26–30, Dowden,* Life, *1886; 41–50 Rogers,* Shelley at Work, *1956.*
  11 Tyrant's] Tyrants *Esd.*   18 Sees] Yet Sees *Esd.*   24 despot's] despots *Esd.*

The voice of blood shall on his crimes call down revenge!   25
  And the spirits of the brave
  Shall start from every grave,
  Whilst, from her Atlantic throne,
  Freedom sanctifies the groan
That fans the glorious fires of its change!   30

  Monarch!—sure employer
    Of vice and want and woe,
  Thou conscienceless destroyer,
    Who and what art thou?—
The dark prison-house that in the dust shall lie,   35
  The pyramid which guilt
  First planned, which Man has built,—
    At whose footstone want and woe
    With a ceaseless murmur flow,
And whose peak attracts the tempests of the sky!   40

  The pyramids shall fall—
    And, Monarchs, so shall ye!
  Thrones shall rust in the hall
    Of forgotten royalty!
Whilst Virtue, Truth and Peace shall arise,   45
  And a Paradise on Earth
  From your fall shall date its birth,
    And human life shall seem
    Like a short and happy dream,
Ere we wake in the daybeam of the skies.   50

25 Shall *over* in *Esd.*

13

ON ROBERT EMMET'S TOMB

February–March 1812

May the tempests of winter that sweep o'er thy tomb
    Disturb not a slumber so sacred as thine!
May the breezes of summer that breathe of perfume
    Waft their balmiest dews to so hallowed a shrine!

May the foot of the tyrant, the coward, the slave,   5
    Be palsied with dread where thine ashes repose!—
Where that undying shamrock still blooms on thy grave
    Which sprung when the dawnlight of Erin arose.

There oft have I marked, the grey gravestones among,
    Where thy relics distinguished in lowliness lay,   10
The peasant boy pensively lingering long,
    ⟨And silently weep as he passed away.⟩

And how could he not pause if the blood of his sires
    Ever wakened one generous throb in his heart?—
How could he inherit a spark of their fires   15
    If tearless and frigid he dared to depart?

Not the scrolls of a court could emblazon thy fame
    Like the silence that reigns in the palace of thee,
Like the whispers that pass of thy dearly-loved name,
    Like the tears of the good, like the groans of the free.   20

TITLE: *Esd. See n.* AUTOGRAPH, TEXT: *Esd.* DATE: *See n.* PRINTED: *21–28,*
Dowden, Life, 1886.
   18 *There is a cross against this line. Perhaps a footnote was intended.*

No trump tells thy virtues—the grave where they rest
  With thy dust shall remain unpolluted by fame,
Till thy foes, by the world and by fortune caressed,
  Shall pass like a mist from the light of thy name.

When the storm-cloud that lowers o'er the daybeam is gone, 25
  Unchanged, unextinguished its life-spring will shine;
When Erin has ceased with their memory to groan
  She will smile through the tears of revival on thine.

14

A TALE OF SOCIETY AS IT IS

FROM FACTS, 1811

1811–12

She was an agèd woman, and the years
  Which she had numbered on her toilsome way
  Had bowed her natural powers to decay.
  She was an agèd woman; yet the ray
Which faintly glimmered through the starting tears,   5
  Pressed from their beds by silent misery,
  Hath soul's imperishable energy.
She was a cripple, and incapable
  To add one mite to golden luxury;
And therefore did her spirit clearly feel   10
  That Poverty, the crime of tainting stain,
Would merge her in the depths never to rise again.

AUTOGRAPH: *Esd.* (*complete*), *BM* (*1–79 only*)   TITLE, TEXT: *Esd.*   DATE: *See n.*
PRINTED: *1–79 from BM, Rossetti, PW, 1870*; *1–79 from a transcript of Esd.,
Ingpen & Peck, Jul. 1927, but see below and Intr. § 8.*
   5 the *Esd.*] her *BM*   6 from their beds *Esd.*] into light *BM* from their
lids *1927*   9 golden *Esd.*] gold-fed *BM*   10 clearly *Esd.*] dimly *BM*
12 the *Esd.*] its *BM*

One only son's love had supported her.
　　She long had struggled with infirmity
　　Lingering from human life-scenes; for to die,　　　　15
　　When Fate has spared to rend some mental tie,
Not many wish and surely fewer dare.
　　But when the tyrant's bloodhounds forced her child
　　For his curst power unhallowed arms to wield,
Bend to another's will, become a thing　　　　　　20
　　More senseless than the sword of battlefield,
Then did she feel keen sorrow's keenest sting,
And many years had passed ere comfort they would bring.

For seven years did this poor woman live
　　In unparticipated solitude.　　　　　　　　　25
　　Thou might'st have seen her in the forest rude
　　Picking the scattered remnants of its wood;
If human thou might'st then have learned to grieve.
　　The gleanings of precarious charity
　　Her scantiness of food did scarce supply,　　　　30
The proofs of an unspeaking sorrow dwelt
　　Within her ghastly hollowness of eye;
Each arrow of the season's change she felt;
　　Yet still she yearned, ere her sad course were run—
One only hope it was—once more to see her son.　　　35

It was an eve of June, when every star
　　Spoke peace from Heaven to those on Earth that live.
　　She rested on the moor. 'Twas such an eve
　　When first her soul began indeed to grieve:
Then he was here—now he is very far.　　　　　40

　　15 from *Esd.*] to *BM, 1927*　　　17 Not *Esd.*] *BM MS torn* Would *1870*
18 her *Esd.*] the *BM*　　　19 his curst *BM*] tyrants *Esd. See n.*　　　23 *would*]
wd. *Esd.* cd. *BM*　　　26 forest *BM*] desart *Esd. See n.*　　　28 grieve *Esd.*]
feel *BM*　　　34 yearned *Esd.*] groans *BM*　　her sad course *Esd.*] yet her race
BM　　　37 to those on Earth that live] *omitted in BM where the line is filled
out by a row of crosses. See n.*

The freshness of the balmy evening
A sorrow o'er her weary soul did fling,
Yet not devoid of rapture's mingled tear;
A balm was in the poison of the sting.
This agèd sufferer for many a year   45
　　Had never felt such comfort. She suppressed
A sigh and, turning round ... clasped William to her breast!

And though his form was wasted by the woe
　　Which despots on their victims love to wreak,
　　Though his sunk eyeball and his faded cheek   50
　　Of slavery, violence and scorn did speak,
Yet did the agèd woman's bosom glow:
　　The vital fire seemed re-illumed within
　　By this sweet unexpected welcoming.
O consummation of the fondest hope   55
　　That ever soared on Fancy's dauntless wing!
O tenderness that foundst so sweet a scope!
　　Prince, who dost swell upon thy mighty sway,—
When thou cans't feel such love thou shalt be great as they!

Her son, compelled, the tyrant's foes had fought,   60
　　Had bled in battle, and the stern control
　　That ruled his sinews and coerced his soul
　　Utterly poisoned life's unmingled bowl,
And unsubduable evils on him wrought.
　　He was the shadow of the lusty child   65
　　Who, when the time of summer season smiled,
For her did earn a meal of honesty,
　　And with affectionate discourse beguiled
　　The keen attacks of pain and poverty,—

41 freshness *Esd.*] sweetness *BM*　　　42 weary *Esd.*] aged *BM*　　　**45** This
Esd.] The *BM*　　　49 despots *Esd.*] tyrants *BM*　　　50 eyeball *Esd. BM*]
eyeballs *1870*　　　51 slavery *Esd. BM*] slavery's *1870*　　　56 dauntless
Esd.] wildest *BM*　　　58 swell upon *Esd.*] pride thee on *BM*　　　59 thou
Esd. BM] *italicized, 1870, 1927*　　　60 tyrant's] tyrants *Esd.*　　　country's
BM　　　62 That *Esd.*] Which *BM*　　　64 wrought *Esd.*] brought *BM*
67 For her did earn *Esd.*] Did earn for her *BM*

Till Power, as envying this her only joy,   70
From her maternal bosom tore the unhappy boy.

And now cold Charity's unwelcome dole
   Was insufficient to support the pair;
   And they would perish rather than would bear
   The law's stern slavery and the insolent stare   75
With which law loves to rend the poor man's soul—
   The bitter scorn, the spirit-sinking noise
   Of heartless mirth which women, men and boys
Wake in this scene of legal misery.
   Oh, William's spirit rather would rejoice   80
On some wild heath with his dear charge to die,—
   The death that keenest penury might give
Were sweeter far than cramped by slavery to live!

And they have borne thus long the winter's cold,
   The driving sleet, the penetrating rain;   85
   It seemeth that their element is pain,
   And that they never will feel life again.
For is it life to be so deathlike old?—
   The sun's kind light feeds every living thing
   That spreads its blossoms to the breath of spring,   90
But who feeds thee, unhappy wanderer?
   With the fat slaves who from the rich man's board
Lick the fallen crumbs thou scantily dost share,
   And mutterest for the gift a heartless prayer;
   The flow'rs fade not thus—thou must poorly die: 95
The changeful year feeds them, the tyrant man feeds thee.

And is it life that in youth's blasted morn
   Not one of youth's dear raptures is enjoyed,—
   All natural bliss with servitude alloyed,
   The beating heart, the sparkling eye destroyed   100
And manhood of its brightest glories shorn?—

70 this her *Esd.*] her this *BM*   74–75 perish . . . stare *underlined*
in BM   92 from *above* [by] *Esd.*   98 is] are *Esd.*

Debased by rapine, drunkenness and woe,
  The foeman's sword, the vulgar tyrant's blow,—
Ruined in body and soul, till heaven arrive,
  His health and peace insultingly laid low?—   105
Without a fear to die or wish to live,
  Withered and sapless, miserably poor,
Relinquished for his wounds to beg from door to door?

See'st thou yon humble sod where osiers bind
  The pillow of the monumentless dead?   110
  There, since her thorny pilgrimage is sped,
  The agèd sufferer rests on the cold bed
Which all who seek or who avoid must find.
  O let her sleep! And there, at close of eve,
  'Twere holiness in solitude to grieve   115
And ponder on the wretchedness of Earth.
  With joy of melancholy I would leave
A spot that to such deep-felt thoughts gives birth,
  And, though I could not pour the useless prayer,
Would weep upon the grave and leave a blessing there. 120

15

THE SOLITARY

1810

Dare'st thou amid this varied multitude
  To live alone, an isolated thing?
  To see the busy beings round thee spring,
And care for none?—in thy calm solitude
A flower that scarce breathes in the desert rude   5
  To Zephyr's passing wing?

TITLE, DATE, TEXT: *Esd.*   AUTOGRAPH: *Esd.*   PRINTED: *apparently from a transcript of Esd., Rossetti,* PW, *1870.*

Not the swarth Pariah in some Indian grove,
  Lone, lean, and hunted by his brothers' hate,
  Hath drunk so deep the cup of bitter fate
As that poor wretch who cannot, cannot love: 10
He bears a load which nothing can remove,
  A killing, withering weight.

He smiles—'tis sorrow's deadliest mockery;
  He speaks—the cold words flow not from his soul;
  He acts like others, drains the genial bowl,—   15
Yet, yet he longs, although he fears, to die;
He pants to reach what yet he seems to fly,
  Dull life's extremest goal.

16

THE MONARCH'S FUNERAL

AN ANTICIPATION

1810

The growing gloom of eventide
  Has quenched the sunbeam's latest glow,
And lowers upon the woe and pride
  That blasts the city's peace below.

At such an hour how sad the sight,—   5
  To mark a Monarch's funeral,
When the dim shades of awful night
  Rest on the coffin's velvet pall!—

TITLE, AUTOGRAPH, DATE, TEXT: *Esd.*
  1 growing *possibly* glowing in *Esd.*, *though the uncertain second letter might
be an anticipation of* glow *in the next line.*   2 sunbeam's] sunbeams *Esd.*,
possibly for sunbeams'

To see the Gothic arches show
　A varied mass of light and shade,   10
While to the torches' crimson glow
　A vast cathedral is displayed!—

To see with what a silence deep
　The thousands o'er this death-scene brood,—
As though some wizard's charm did creep   15
　Upon the countless multitude!—

To see this awful pomp of death
　For one frail mass of mouldering clay,
When nobler men the tomb beneath
　Have sunk unwept, unseen away!   20

For who was he, the uncoffined slain
　That fell in Erin's injured isle,
Because his spirit dared disdain
　To light his country's funeral pile?

Shall he not ever live in lays   25
　The warmest that a Muse may sing,
Whilst monumental marbles raise
　The fame of a departed King?

May not the Muse's darling theme
　Gather its glorious garland thence,   30
Whilst some frail tombstone's dotard dream
　Fades with a Monarch's impotence?

—Yet 'tis a scene of wondrous awe
　To see a coffined Monarch lay,
That the wide grave's insatiate maw   35
　Be glutted with a regal prey!

Who *now* shall public councils guide?
   Who rack the poor, on gold to dine?
Who waste the means of regal pride
   For which a million wretches pine?   40

It is a child of earthly breath,
   A being perishing as he,
Who, throned in yonder pomp of death,
   Hath now fulfilled his destiny.

Now dust to dust restore, O Pride!—   45
   Unmindful of thy fleeting power,
Whose empty confidence has vied
   With human life's most treacherous hour,

One moment feel that in the breast
   With regal crimes and troubles vext   50
The pampered earthworms soon will rest,—
   One moment feel—and die the next!

Yet deem not in the tomb's control
   The vital lamp of life can fail,—
Deem not that e'er the Patriot's soul   55
   Is wasted by the withering gale!

The dross which forms the *King* is gone
   And reproductive earth supplies,—
As senseless as the clay and stone
   In which the kindred body lies;   60

The soul which makes the *Man* doth soar,
   And love alone survives to shed
All that its tide of bliss can pour
   Of Heaven upon the blessed dead.

45 restore, O Pride!—] restore! . . . O Pride *Esd. See n.*

So shall the sun for ever burn,   65
   So shall the midnight lightnings die,
And joy that glows at Nature's bourne
   Outlive terrestrial misery.

And will the crowd who silent stoop
   Around the lifeless Monarch's bier,   70
A mournful and dejected group,
   Breathe not one sigh, or shed one tear?

Ah, no! 'Tis wonder, 'tis not woe,—
   Even royalists might groan to see
The *Father of the People* so   75
   Lost in the Sacred Majesty!

17

TO THE REPUBLICANS OF NORTH AMERICA
February 1812

Brothers! between you and me
   Whirlwinds sweep and billows roar,
Yet in spirit oft I see
   On the wild and winding shore
Freedom's bloodless banner wave,—   5
Feel the pulses of the brave
Unextinguished by the grave,—
   See them drenched in sacred gore,—
Catch the patriot's gasping breath
Murmuring 'Liberty in death!'   10

AUTOGRAPH: *Esd. (complete)*, *BM (1–30, 41–50)*   TEXT: *Esd.*   TITLE, DATE:
See n. PRINTED: *1–30, 41–50, from BM, Rossetti, PW, 1870; 1–30, 41–50, from
a transcript of Esd., Ingpen & Peck, Jul. 1927, but see below and Intr. § 8.*
  4 the *Esd.*] thy *BM*   5 banner *Esd.*] banners *BM, 1927*   7 by
Esd.] in *BM*   9 patriot's *1870*] patriots *Esd.* warriors *BM*   10 'Liberty
1870] Liberty *Esd., BM, 1927* in *Esd.*] or *BM, 1927*   death!'] death *Esd.,
BM*, 'death!' *1927*

Shout aloud! Let every slave
    Crouching at Corruption's throne
Start into a man, and brave
    Racks and chains without a groan!—
Let the castle's heartless glow   15
And the hovel's vice and woe
Fade like gaudy flowers that blow,
    Weeds that peep and then are gone!—
Whilst, from misery's ashes risen,
Love shall burst the captive's prison.   20

Cotopaxi! bid the sound
    Through thy sister mountains ring,
Till each valley smile around
    At the blissful welcoming!
And, O thou stern Ocean-deep,   25
Whose eternal billows sweep
Shores where thousands wake to weep
    Whilst they curse some villain king,
On the winds that fan thy breast
    Bear thou news of Freedom's rest!   30

Earth's remotest bounds shall start,
    Every despot's bloated cheek,
Pallid as his bloodless heart,
    Frenzy woe and dread shall speak;
Blood may fertilise the tree   35
Of new-bursting Liberty,—
Let the guiltiness then be
    On the slaves that ruin wreak,
On the unnatural tyrant-brood,
    Slow to peace and swift to blood.   40

15 castle's *BM*] castles *Esd*.   16 hovel's] hovels *Esd. BM*   20 captive's] Captives *Esd. BM* Captive *1927*   26 Whose eternal *Esd.*] Thou whose foamy *BM*   28 some *Esd.* a *BM*

  Can the daystar dawn of love
   Where the flag of war unfurled
  Floats with crimson stain above
   Such a desolated world?—
  Never! but, to vengeance driven,   45
  When the patriot's spirit shriven
  Seeks in death its native Heaven,
   Then, to speechless horror hurled,
  Widowed Earth may balm the bier
  Of its memory with a tear.   50

18

WRITTEN AT CWM ELAN

[July–August] 1811

When the peasant hies him home and the day-planet reposes,
 Pillowed on the azure peaks that bound the western sight,
When each mountain flower its modest petal tremulously
  closes,
 And sombre, shrouded Twilight comes to lead her sister
  Night,—
Vestal dark! how dear to me are then thy dews of lightness, 5
That bathe my brow so withering, scorched beneath the day-
  beam's brightness,—
More dear to me, though Day be robed in vest of dazzling
  whiteness,
 Is one folding of the garment dusk that wraps thy form,
  O Night!

∧ 44 The fabric of a ruined world *BM* 48 There to desolation hurled *BM*
49 Earth may balm *Esd.*] love may watch *BM* earth may watch *1927*
50 Balm thee with its dying tear *BM, 1927*

∨ TITLE, AUTOGRAPH, TEXT: *Esd.* DATE: *See n.*
 6 daybeam's] daybeams *Esd.*

With thee I still delight to sit where dizzy Danger slumbers,
  Where 'mid the rocks the fitful blast hath waked its wild-
    est lay,   10
Till beneath the yellow moonbeam decay the dying numbers,
  And Silence, even in Fancy's throne, hath seized again the
    sway.
Again she must resign it—hark! For wildest cadence pouring,
Far, far amid the viewless glen beneath the Elan roaring,
'Mid tangèd woods and shapeless rocks with moonlight sum-
    mits soaring,   15
  It mingles its magic murmuring with the blast that floats
    away.

19

TO DEATH

1810

  Death! where is thy victory?
    To triumph whilst I die?—
  To triumph whilst thine ebon wing
    Enfolds my shuddering soul?
  O Death! where is thy sting?   5
    Not when the tides of murder roll,
When Nations groan that Kings may bask in bliss,
Death, could'st thou boast a victory such as this!—
    When, in his hour
    Of pomp and power,   10

∧ 14 glen *above* [rocks] *Esd.*   15 tangèd] tangued *Esd. See n.*

∨ AUTOGRAPH: *Esd.* (*complete*), *Pf.* (*1–48*) TEXT, TITLE: *Esd.* DATE: *See n.*
PRINTED: *1–48 from Pf., Hogg,* Life, *1858. For text in Jul. 1927, see below and*
Intr. § 8.
    3 ebon wing *Esd.*] ebon wing *above* [hand of fate] *Pf.*   6 when *Esd. Pf.*]
where *1927*   8 couldst *Esd.*] canst *Pf.*   9–10 *a single line in Pf.*

Thy slave, the mightiest murderer, gave
   'Mid Nature's cries,
    The sacrifice
Of myriads to glut the grave,—
When sunk the tyrant, sensualism's slave,   15
Or Freedom's life-blood streamed upon thy shrine,—
Stern despot, could'st thou boast a victory such as mine?

   To know in dissolution's void
    That earthly hopes and fears decay,
  That every sense but Love, destroyed   20
    Must perish with its kindred clay—
     Perish Ambition's crown,
     Perish its sceptred sway,—
From Death's pale front fade Pride's fastidious frown,
In Death's damp vault the lurid fires decay   25
Which Envy lights at heaven-born Virtue's beam—
    That all the cares subside
    Which lurk beneath the tide
    Of life's unquiet stream,—
    Yes! this were victory!   30
And on some rock whose dark form glooms the sky
  To stretch these pale limbs when the soul is fled,—
To baffle the lean passions of their prey,
  To sleep within the chambers of the dead!—
    Oh, not the wretch, around whose dazzling throne 35
His countless courtiers mock the words they say,
    Triumphs amid the bud of glory blown
As I on Death's last pang and faint expiring groan!

---

11 Thy slave *Esd.*] Thy blow *Pf.* His blow *1858*   12–13 *a single line in* **Pf.**
14 myriads *Esd.*] millions *Pf.*   15 sensualism's *Esd.*] desolation's *Pf.*
17 despot *Esd.*] tyrant *Pf.*   19 That earthly *Esd.*] That mortals *Pf.*   hopes
and fears *Esd.*] bubbles sank *above* [hopes and fears] *Pf.*   decay *Esd.*] away
Pf.   20 sense *Esd.*] thing *Pf.*   23 its *Esd.*] her *Pf.*   26 Which
Esd.] That *Pf.*   30 were *Esd.*] is *Pf. 1927*   31 some *Esd.*] yon
Pf.   32 when *Esd. Pf.*] where *1927*   34 chambers *Esd.*] palace *Pf. 1927*
35 wretch *Esd.*] King *Pf.*   38 on Death's last pang *Esd.*] in this cold bed
Pf. 1927

Tremble, ye Kings, whose luxury mocks the woe
That props the column of unnatural state!—   40
    Ye the curses, deep though low,
    From Misery's tortured breast that flow,
      Shall usher to your fate.
Tremble, ye conquerors, at whose fell command
  The War-Fiend riots o'er an happy land!   45
    Ye Desolation's gory throng
    Shall bear from victory along
    To Death's mysterious strand.
'Twere Hell that Vice no pain should know
  But every scene that Memory gives,   50
Though from the self-same fount might flow
  The joy which Virtue aye receives.
It is the grave,—no conqueror triumphs now;
  The wreaths of bay that bound his head
Wither around his fleshless brow,—   55
    Where is the mockery fled
    That fired the tyrant's gaze?
'Tis like the fitful glare that plays
On some dark-rolling thunder-cloud,—
    Plays whilst the thunders roar   60
    But, when the storm is past,
    Fades like the warrior's name.
Death! in thy vault when Kings and peasants lie,
Not Power's stern rod nor Fame's most thrilling blasts
Can liberate thy captives from decay,—   65
My triumph their defeat, my joy their shame,
  Welcome then, peaceful Death! I'll sleep with thee,—
  Mine be thy quiet home, and thine my Victory!

39 Kings *Esd.*] proud *Pf.*   luxury *Esd.*] grandeur *over* [bosoms] *Pf.*
40 That *Esd.*] Which *Pf.*   the] Thy *Esd. Pf.*   41 curses, deep though
low *Esd.*] plainings faint & low *Pf.*   42 breast *Esd.*] soul *above* [breast] *Pf.*
45 happy *Esd.*] peaceful *Pf.*   47 from victory *Esd.*] victorious *Pf.*
48 Death's *Esd.*] that *Pf.*   49 Hell *possibly* well   64 Not *over* [Can] *Esd.*
nor] or *Esd.*   65 Can liberate *Thus, apparently, Esd., though ink is smudged.*

20

'DARK SPIRIT OF THE DESERT RUDE...'

July–August 1811

Dark Spirit of the desert rude,
That o'er this awful solitude,
Each tangled and untrodden wood,
   Each dark and silent glen below,
   Where sunlight's gleamings never glow,   5
Whilst, jetty, musical and still
In darkness speeds the mountain rill,—
   That o'er yon broken peaks sublime,
   Wild shapes that mock the scythe of Time,
And the pure Elan's foamy course   10
Wavest thy wand of magic force,—
   Art thou yon sooty and fearful fowl
That flaps its wing o'er the leafless oak—
   That o'er the dismal scene doth scowl
And mocketh music with ⟨its⟩ croak?   15

I've sought thee where day's beams decay
   On the peak of the lonely hill;
I've sought thee where they melt away
   By the wave of the pebbly rill;
I've strained to catch thy murky form   20
Bestride the rapid and gloomy storm,—
   Thy red and sullen eyeball's glare
   Has shot in a dream through the midnight air,
But never did thy shape express
Such an emphatic gloominess.   25

And where art thou, O thing of gloom?—
On Nature's unreviving tomb,

AUTOGRAPH, TEXT: *Esd.*   DATE: *See n.*
  15 ⟨its⟩ *conjectural: tangled over-writing in Esd.*

Where sapless, blasted and alone
She mourns her blooming centuries gone!
From the fresh sod the violets peep,   30
The buds have burst their frozen sleep,
   Whilst every green and peopled tree
Is alive with Earth's sweet melody.
   But thou alone art here
Thou, desolate oak, whose scathèd head,   35
   For ages has never tremblèd
Whose giant trunk dead lichens bind,
Moaningly sighing in the wind,
With huge loose rocks beneath thee spread,
   Thou, thou alone art here!   40
Remote from every living thing
   Tree, shrub or grass or flower,
Thou seemest of this spot the King,
   And, with a regal power,
⟨Suck⟩, like that race, all sap away,   45
And yet upon the spoil ⟨decay⟩.

21

[REALITY]

1812–13

There is no work, nor device, nor knowledge, nor
wisdom, in the grave, whither thou goest.
                  Ecclesiastes ix. 10

The pale, the cold, and the moony smile
   Which the meteor beam of a starless night
Sheds on a lonely and sea-girt isle,
   Ere the dawning of morn's undoubted light,

∧ 44 And *above* [that] *Esd.*   45–46 *See n.*
∨ TITLE: *Lacking in Esd. and Shelley's printing. See n.*   DATE: *See n.*   AUTO-
GRAPH: *Esd.*   PRINTED: *Shelley, with* Alastor, *1816*   TEXT: *1816*
  2 starless *1816*] stormy *Esd.*   4 Ere *1816*] Till *Esd.*

Is the flame of life so fickle and wan   5
That flits round our steps till their strength is gone.

O man! hold thee on in courage of soul
   Through the stormy shades of thy wordly way,
And the billows of cloud that around thee roll
   Shall sleep in the light of a wondrous day,   10
Where hell and heaven shall leave thee free
To the universe of destiny.

This world is the nurse of all we know,
   This world is the mother of all we feel,
And the coming of death is a fearful blow   15
   To a brain unencompassed with nerves of steel;
When all that we know, or feel, or see,
Shall pass like an unreal mystery.

The secret things of the grave are there,
   Where all but this frame must surely be,   20
Though the fine-wrought eye and the wondrous ear
   No longer will live to hear or to see
All that is great and all that is strange
In the boundless realm of unending change.

Who telleth a tale of unspeaking death?   25
   Who lifteth the veil of what is to come?
Who painteth the shadows that are beneath
   The wide-winding caves of the peopled tomb?

5 flame *1816*] taper *Esd.*   7 in *1816*] with *Esd.*   8 Thro the long
long night of thy doubtful way *Esd.*
10–12   Shall subside in the calm of eternal day
                  For all in this world we can surely know
                  Is a little delight and a little woe   *Esd.*
13–14   All we behold we feel that we know
                  All we percieve we know that we feel   *Esd.*
16 with nerves *1816*] by nervestrings *Esd.*   17 or feel, or see *1816*] we feel
& we see *Esd.*   18 pass *1816*] fleet by *Esd.*   20 frame *1816*] body *Esd.*
23 great *1816*] bright *Esd.*   24 boundless realm *1816*] gradual path
Esd.   25 a tale *1816*] the tales *Esd.*   27 shadows *1816*] beings *Esd.*
28 wide-winding caves *1816*] wide stretching realms *Esd.*

Or uniteth the hopes of what shall be
With the fears and the love for that which we see? 30

22

'DEATH-SPURNING ROCKS...'

? July–August 1811
? June–July 1812

Death-spurning rocks! Here have ye towered since Time
  Sprung from Tradition's mist-encircled height,
Which Memory's palsied pinion dreads to climb
  Awed by the phantoms of its beamless night,—
    Death-spurning rocks! Each jagged form 5
    Shall still arrest the passing storm,
      Whilst, rooted there, the agèd oak
      Is shivered by the lightning's stroke;
  Years shall fade fast and centuries roll away,—
Ye shall spurn death no more but like your oak decay! 10

A maniac-sufferer soared with wild intent
  Where Nature formed these wonders. On the way
There is a little spot . . . Fiends would relent
  Knew they the snares that there for Memory lay,—
    How many a hope and many a fear, 15
    And many a vain and bitter tear;
      Whilst each prophetic feeling wakes
      A brood of mad and venomed snakes
  To make the lifesprings of his soul their food,
To twine around his veins and fatten on his blood! 20

∧ 29 Or *1816*] And *Esd.*
∨ AUTOGRAPH, TEXT: *Esd.*   DATE: *See n.*
  11 A *over* The *apparently in Esd.*   14 snares *above* [pangs] *Esd.* 20
[veins] viens *above* [nerves] *Esd*

To quench his pangs he fled to the wild moor.
  One fleeting beam flashed but its gloom to show,—
Turned was the way-worn wanderer from the door
  Where Pity's self promised to soothe his woe.
    Shall he ⟨turn⟩ back? The tempest there   25
    Sweeps fiercely through the turbid air,
      Beyond a gulf before that yawns,
      The day-star shines, the daybeam dawns,—
God! Nature! Chance!—Remit this misery,—
It burns!—Why need he live to weep who does not fear to
  die?   30

23

THE TOMBS

February–March 1812

These are the tombs. O cold and silent Death,
Thy kingdom and thy subjects here I see!—
  The record of thy victories
  Is graven on every speaking stone
    That marks what once was man.   5

These are the tombs. Am I, who sadly gaze
On the corruption and the skulls around,
  To sum the mass of loathsomeness,
  And to a mound of mouldering flesh,
    Say: 'Thou wert human life'?   10

∧ 25 turn *Shelley seems to have written* fal, *converted the first two letters to* tu, *and added* n, *though failing to convert the third letter very well.*

∨ TITLE, AUTOGRAPH, TEXT: *Esd.* DATE: *See n.* PRINTED: *14–15, Dowden, Life, 1886.*
  3 thy] the *Esd.*

In thee once throbbed the Patriot's beating heart,
In thee once lived the Poet's soaring soul,
   The pulse of love, the calm of thought,
   Courage and charity and truth,
     And high devotedness;   15

All that could sanctify the meanest deeds,
All that might give a manner and a form
   To matter's speechless elements,
   To every brute and morbid shape
     Of this phantasmal world,—   20

⟨That the high sense which from the stern rebuke
Of Erin's victim patriot's death-soul shone
   When blood and chains defiled the land
   Lives in the torn uprooted heart
     His savage murderers burn⟩.   25

Ah, no! Else, while these tombs before me stand,
My soul would hate the coming of its hour,
   Nor would the hopes of life and love
   Be mingled with those fears of death
     That chill the warmest heart.   30

24

TO HARRIET [SHELLEY]

1811–12

It is not blasphemy to hope that Heaven
More perfectly will give those nameless joys
Which throb within the pulses of the blood
And sweeten all that bitterness which Earth

⋀ 19 every *above* [all the] *Esd.*   22 patriot's] patriots *Esd.*
21–25 *See n.*

⋁ TITLE, AUTOGRAPH, TEXT: *Esd.* PRINTED: *58–69 Shelley, 1813, in Note on*
Q. Mab, *viii. 203–7; 1–end, Dowden, Life, 1886.*

Infuses in the heaven-born soul. O thou   5
Whose dear love gleamed upon the gloomy path
Which this lone spirit travelled, drear and cold,
Yet swiftly leading to those awful limits
Which mark the bounds of Time and of the space
When Time shall be no more; wilt thou not turn   10
Those spirit-beaming eyes and look on me,
Until I be assured that Earth is Heaven,
And Heaven is Earth?—will not thy glowing cheek,
Glowing with soft suffusion, rest on mine,
And breathe magnetic sweetness through the frame 15
Of my corporeal nature, through the soul
Now knit with these fine fibres? I would give
The longest and the happiest day that fate
Has marked on my existence but to feel
One soul-reviving kiss . . . O thou most dear,   20
'Tis an assurance that this Earth is Heaven,
And Heaven the flower of that untainted seed
Which springeth here beneath such love as ours.
Harriet! let death all mortal ties dissolve,
But ours shall not be mortal! The cold hand   25
Of Time may chill the love of earthly minds
Half frozen now; the frigid intercourse
Of common souls lives but a summer's day;
It dies, where it arose, upon this earth.
But ours! oh, 'tis the stretch of Fancy's hope   30
To portray its continuance as now,
Warm, tranquil, spirit-healing. Nor when age
Has tempered these wild ecstasies, and given
A soberer tinge to the luxurious glow
Which blazing on devotion's pinnacle   35
Makes virtuous passion supersede the power
Of reason; nor when life's aestival sun
To deeper manhood shall have ripened me;

32–52 *See nn.*   32 spirit-healing. Nor *Esd.*] spirit-healing; nor *1886 & edd.*
40 sweetness—] sweetness, *Esd.*

Nor when some years have added judgement's store
To all thy woman sweetness—all the fire   40
Which throbs in thine enthusiast heart,—not then
Shall holy friendship (for what other name
May love like ours assume?),—not even then
Shall Custom so corrupt, or the cold forms
Of this desolate world so harden us   45
That, when we think of the dear love that binds
Our souls in soft communion while we know
Each other's thoughts and feelings, we can say
Unblushingly a heartless compliment,
Praise, hate, or love with the unthinking world,   50
Or dare to cut the unrelaxing nerve
That knits our love to virtue. Can those eyes,
Beaming with mildest radiance on my heart
To purify its purity, e'er bend
To soothe its vice or consecrate its fears?   55
Never, thou second Self! Is confidence
So vain in virtue that I learn to doubt
The mirror even of Truth? Dark flood of Time,
Roll as it listeth; I measure not
By months or moments thy ambiguous course.   60
Another may stand by me on thy brink,
And watch the bubble whirled beyond his ken,
Which pauses at my feet. The sense of love,
The thirst for action, and the impassioned thought
Prolong my being; if I wake no more,   65
My life more actual living will contain
Than some grey veteran's of the world's cold school,
Whose listless hours unprofitably roll
By one enthusiast feeling unredeemed.
Virtue and Love! unbending Fortitude,   70
Freedom, Devotedness and Purity—
That life my Spirit consecrates to you!

41 heart,—] heart, *Esd.* heart; *1886 & edd.*   43 assume?),—] assume?) *Esd.*
assume?), *1886 & edd.*   46, 48 That, . . . we can] As . . . can we *Esd. 1886*
& edd.   47 communion] communion, *Esd. 1886 & edd.*

25

SONNET

TO HARRIET [SHELLEY] ON HER BIRTHDAY

1 August 1812

O thou whose radiant eyes and beamy smile,
    Yet even a sweeter somewhat indexing,
Have known full many an hour of mine to guile,
    Which else would only bitter memories bring:
O ever thus, thus, as on this natal day,   5
    Though Age's frost may blight those tender eyes,
    Destroy that kindling cheek's transparent dyes,
And those luxuriant tresses change to grey—
    Ever as now with Love and Virtue's glow
May thine unwithering soul not cease to burn,—   10
    Still may thine heart with those pure thoughts o'erflow
Which force from mine such quick and warm return!
    And I must love thee even more than this,
Nor doubt that thou and I part but to meet in bliss.

26

SONNET

TO A BALLOON LADEN WITH *KNOWLEDGE*

August 1812

Bright ball of flame that through the gloom of even
    Silently takest thine aethereal way,
    And with surpassing glory dimm'st each ray
Twinkling amid the dark blue depths of Heaven,—

⋀ TITLE, AUTOGRAPH, TEXT, DATE: *Esd.* PRINTED: *9–12, Dowden,* Life, *1886.*
⋁ AUTOGRAPH, TEXT: *Esd.* TITLE: *Esd. See n.* DATE: *See n.* PRINTED: *Dowden,* Life, *1886.*

Unlike the fire thou bearest, soon shalt thou   5
Fade like a meteor in surrounding gloom,
   Whilst that, unquenchable, is doomed to glow
A watch-light by the patriot's lonely tomb;
   A ray of courage to the oppressed and poor;
A spark, though gleaming on the hovel's hearth,   10
   Which through the tyrant's gilded domes shall roar;
A beacon in the darkness of the Earth;
   A sun which, o'er the renovated scene,
   Shall dart like Truth where Falsehood yet has been.

27

SONNET

ON LAUNCHING SOME BOTTLES FILLED WITH *KNOWLEDGE* INTO THE BRISTOL CHANNEL

August 1812

Vessels of heavenly medicine! May the breeze
   Auspicious waft your dark green forms to shore;
   Safe may ye stem the wide surrounding roar
Of the wild whirlwinds and the raging seas;
   And oh! if Liberty e'er deigned to stoop   5
From yonder lowly throne her crownless brow,
   Sure she will breathe around your emerald group
The fairest breezes of her West that blow,
   Yes! she will waft ye to some freeborn soul
Whose eye-beam, kindling as it meets your freight,   10
   Her heaven-born flame on suffering Earth will light,
Until its radiance gleams from pole to pole,

⋀ 11 tyrant's] tyrants *Esd.*

⋁ AUTOGRAPH, TEXT: *Esd.*   TITLE: *Esd. See n. on No. 26*   DATE: *See n.*
PRINTED: *Dowden*, Life, *1886.*
   3 stem *thus 1886, and preferred here, though Esd. might read* stern   8 West
1904] west *Esd. 1886*   11 on] in *1886*

And tyrant-hearts with powerless envy burst
To see their night of ignorance dispersed.

28

SONNET

ON WAITING FOR A WIND
TO CROSS THE BRISTOL CHANNEL
FROM DEVONSHIRE TO WALES

August 1812

Oh, for the South's benign and balmy breeze!
   Come, gentle Spirit! Through the wide Heaven sweep:
Chase inauspicious Boreas from the seas,
   That gloomy tyrant of the unwilling deep!
These wilds, where Man's profane and tainting hand   5
   Nature's primaeval loveliness has marred
   And some few souls of the high bliss debarred
Which else obey her powerful command,
   I leave without a sigh; ye mountain piles
That load in grandeur Cambria's emerald vales,   10
   Whose sides are fair in cultivation's smiles,
Around whose jagged heads the storm-cloud sails,—
   A heart that's all thine own receive in me
   With Nature's fervour ⟨fraught⟩ and calm in ⟨purity⟩!

TITLE, AUTOGRAPH, TEXT: *Esd.* DATE: *See n.* PRINTED: *5–10, partially,*
Dowden, Life, *1886.*
   13 ⟨receive⟩ recieves *Esd.*   14 ⟨fraught⟩ *conjectural: the last four*
letters seem clear. ⟨purity⟩ *conjectural: possibly* piety—*the last two letters seem*
clear.

29

TO HARRIET [SHELLEY]

1811–12

Harriet! thy kiss to my soul is dear,—
　　At evil or pain I would never repine
If to every sigh and to every tear
　　Were added a look and a kiss of thine.
Nor is it the look when it glances fire,　　　　　　　　5
　　Nor the kiss when bathed in the dew of delight,
Nor the throb of the heart when it pants desire
　　From the shadows of eve to the morning light,

But the look when a lustre of joy-mingled woe
　　Has faintly obscured all its bliss-beaming Heaven—　　10
Such a lovely, benign and enrapturing glow
　　As sunset can paint on the clouds of even—
And a kiss, which the languish of silent love,
　　Though eloquent, faints with the toil of expressing,
Yet so light that thou canst not refuse, my dove,　　　15
　　To add this one to the debt of caressing.

Harriet! adieu to all vice and care,—
　　Thy love is my heaven, thy arms are my world!
While thy kiss and thy look to my soul remain dear
　　I should smile though Earth from its base be hurled:　20
For a heart as pure and a mind as free
　　As ever gave lover to thee I give,
And all that I ask in return from thee
　　Is to love like me and with me to live.

TITLE, AUTOGRAPH, TEXT: *Esd.*　DATE: *See Intr. § 7.*

This heart that beats for thy love and bliss,   25
    Harriet, beats for its country too;
And it never would thrill with thy look or kiss
    If it dared to that country's cause be untrue.
Honour and wealth and life it spurns,
    But thy love is a prize it is sure to gain,   30
And the heart that with love and virtue burns
    Will never repine at evil or pain.

30

MARY TO THE SEA-WIND

? *c.* 1812–13

I implore thee, I implore thee, softly-swelling breeze,
    Waft swift the sail of my lover to the shore,
That under the shadow of yon darkly-woven trees
    I may meet him, I may meet him, to part with him no more.

For this boon, for this boon, sweet Sea-Wind, will I weave 5
    A garland wild of heath flowers to breathe to thee perfume;
Thou wilt kiss them yet, like Henry's, thy kisses will but leave
    A more heaven-breathing fragrance and sense-enchanting
        bloom.

And then on summer evens I will hasten to inhale,
    Remembering that thou wert so kind thy balmy, balmy
        breath,   10
And when thy tender pinions in the gloom begin to fail,
    I will catch thee to my bosom ere thou diest on the heath.

I will catch thee to my bosom—and, if Henry's oaths are true,
    A softer, sweeter grave thou wilt never find than there;
Nor is it lovely Sea-Wind, nor is it to undo   15
    That my arms are so inviting, that my bosom is so fair.

TITLE, AUTOGRAPH, TEXT: *Esd.*   DATE: *See n.*

811450   E

A RETROSPECT OF TIMES OF OLD

August 1812

The mansions of the Kings are tenantless,—
   Low lie in dust their glory and their shame!
No tongue survives their virtuous deeds to bless,—
   No tongue with execration blasts their fame!
But on some ruined pile, where yet the gold[1]   5
Casts purple brilliance o'er colossal snow,
Where sapphire eyes in breathing statues glow,
And the tainted blast sighs 'mid the reeds below,
Where grim effigies of the Gods of old
   In mockery stand of ever-changing men   10
   (Their ever-changing worship, ah, how vain!
Yet baubles aye must please the multitude!)—
There Desolation dwells. . . . Where are the Kings?
   Why sleep they now if sleep be not eternal?
   Cannot Oblivion's silent tauntings call   15
The Kings and Heroes from their quietude
   Of Death, to snatch the scrolls from her palsying hand
To tell the world how mighty once they were? . . .
They dare not wake . . . thy victory is here
   O Death! . . . yet I hear unearthly voices cry   20
'Death, thou'lt be swallowed up in victory!'

Yes, dream of fame! The halls are desolate
   Where whitened skeletons of thine heroes lie;

---

[1] Gilding yet remains on the cornices of the ruined palaces of Persepolis. [*Shelley's footnote.*]

TITLE, AUTOGRAPH, TEXT: *Esd.* DATE: *See n.* PRINTED: *71–83, Rogers,* Shelley at Work, *1956.*
    11–12   Thier ever changing worship ah how vain!
                (Yet baubles aye must please the multitude) *Esd. See n.*
22 Dream of fame! *over* [?] brilliant piles

Stillness keeps watch before each grass-grown gate,
   Save where, amid thy towers, the simoon's sigh   25
Wakes the lone lyre whose mistress sleeps below,
And bids it thrill to notes of awfulness and woe.

Here, ages since, some royal bloodhound crept,
   When on these pillared piles a midnight lay
Which but from visioned memories long has fled,   30
To work ambition whilst his brother slept
   And, reckless of the peaceful smile that played
   Around his dream-fraught features when, betrayed,
   They told each innocent secret of the day,
Wakened the thoughtless victim, bade him stare   35
   Upon the murderous steel ... The chaste, pale glare
Of the midnight moonbeam kissed its glittering blade
   A moment and, its brightness quenched in blood,
   Distained with murder the moon's silver flood!
The blushing moon wide-gathering vapours shrouded; 40
   One moment did he triumph,—but remorse,
Suspicion, anguish, fear all triumph clouded—
   Destruction, suicide, his last resource!—
Wide yawned the torrent,—the moon's stormy flash
Disclosed its black tumultuousness—the crash   45
   Of rocks and boughs mixed with its roarings hoarse:
A moment, and he dies! Hark to the awful dash!

Such were thy works, Ambition, even amid
   The darksome times of generations gone
Which the dark veil of viewless hours has hid,   50
   The veil of hours for ever onward flown.[1]

[1] I believe it was only in those early times when Monarchy was in its apprenticeship that its compunction for evil deeds was unendurable. There is no instance upon record parallel to that related above, but I know that neither men nor sets of men become vicious but slowly, and step by step, each less difficult than the former. [*Shelley's footnote.*]

44 Wide] *Shelley seems to have written, unmetrically,* wider *and attempted to delete the last letter.*

Swift roll the waves of Time's eternal tide,
    The peasant's grave, marked by no tribute stone,
Not less remembered than the gilded bed
    In which the hero slept,—now ever gone   55
        Passion and will and power, flesh, heart and brain and
            bone!

Each trophied bust, where gore-emblazoned Victory
    In breathing marble shook the ensanguined spear,
Flinging its heavy purple canopy
    In cold expanse o'er martyred Freedom's bier,—   60
Each gorgeous altar where the victims bled
    And grim Gods frowned above their human prey,—
Where the high temple echoing to the yell
    Of death-pangs, to the long and shuddering groan,
Whilst sacred hymns along the aisles did swell   65
    And pitiless priests drowned each discordant moan,—
All, all have faded in past time away!
    New gods, like men, changing in ceaseless flow,
Ever at hand as ancient ones decay,
    Heroes and kings and laws have plunged the world in
        woe!   70

Sesostris, Caesar, and Pizarro,—come!
Thou, Moses, and Mahommed,[1]—leave that gloom!
    Destroyers, never shall your memory die!
Approach, pale Phantom, to yon mouldering tomb
    Where all thy bones, hopes, crimes, and passions lie! 75
And thou, poor peasant, when thou pass'st the grave
    Where, deep enthroned in monumental pride,
Sleep low in dust the mighty and the brave,
    Where the mad conqueror, whose gigantic stride

[1] To this innumerable list of legal murderers our own age affords numerous
addenda. Frederic of Prussia, Buonaparte, Suvoroff, Wellington and Nelson
are the most skilful and notorious scourges of their species of the present day.
[*Shelley's footnote.*]

The Earth was too confined for, doth abide,   80
    Housing his bones amid a little clay,—
In gratitude to Nature's Spirit bend,
And wait in still hope for thy better end.

32

THE VOYAGE

August 1812

    Quenched is old Ocean's rage:
    Each horrent wave, that flung
Its neck that writhed beneath the tempest's scourge
    Indignant up to Heaven,
    Now breathes in its sweet slumber   5
    To mingle with the day
    A spirit of tranquillity.
    Beneath the cloudless sun
    The gently swelling main
    Scatters a thousand colourings;   10
And the wind, that wanders vaguely through the void,
With the flapping of the sail, and the dashing at the prow,
And the whistle of the sailor in that shadow of a calm
    A ravishing harmony makes.
Oh, why is a rapt soul e'er recalled   15
    From the palaces of visioned bliss
    To the cells of real sorrow?

    That little vessel's company
    Beheld the sight of loveliness:
    The dark grey rocks that towered   20
    Above the slumbering sea,
    And their reflected forms

TITLE, AUTOGRAPH, DATE, TEXT: *Esd.*   PRINTED: *40–62, 102–111, Rogers,*
Shelley at Work, *1956.*

Deep in its faintly-waving mirror given;
   They heard the low breeze sighing
   The listless sails and ropes among,   25
   They heard the music at the prow,
     And the hoarse, distant clash
     Sent from yon gloomy caves
Where Earth and Ocean strive for mastery.

   A mingled mass of feeling   30
   Those human spirits pressed,
   As they heard, and saw, and felt
   Some fancied fear, and some real woe
   Mixed with those glimpses of heavenly joy
     That dawned on each passive soul.   35
   Where is the woe that never sees
   One joybeam illumine the night of the mind?
     Where is the bliss that never feels
   One dart from the quiver of earthly pain?

   The young and happy spirits now   40
   Along the world are voyaging;
   Love, friendship, virtue, truth,
   Simplicity of sentiment and speech,
     And other sensibilities
   Known by no outward name—   45
   Some faults that Love forgives,
   Some flaws that Friendship shares;
   Hearts passionate and benevolent,
   Alive, and urgent to repair
   The errors of their brother heads—   50
     All voyage with them too.
   They look to land, they look to sea,—
   Bounded one is, and palpable
   Even as a noonday scene,
   The other indistinct and dim,   55
   Spangled with dizzying sunbeams,

Boundless, untrod by human step,
Like the vague blisses of a midnight dream,
  Or Death's immeasurable main,
Whose lovely islands gleam at intervals   60
Upon the Spirit's visioned solitude
Through Earth's wide-woven and many-coloured veil.

  It is a moveless calm.
  The sailor's whistle shrill
Speeds clearly through the sleeping atmosphere,—   65
As country curates pray for rain
When drought has frustrated full long
He whistles for a wind
With just the same success.
  Two honest souls were they,   70
And oft had braved in fellowship the storm,
  Till, from that fellowship, had sprung
  A sense of right and liberty
Unbending, undismayed,—aye, they had seen
  Where danger, death and terror played   75
  With human lives in the boiling deep;
  And they had seen the scattered spray
  Of the green and jagged mountain-wave,
  Hid in the lurid tempest-cloud
With lightnings tinging all its fleeting form,   80
  Rolled o'er their fragile bark.
  A dread and hopeless month
  Had they participated once
  In that diminutive bark,—
Their tearless eyes uplifted unto Heaven   85
  So fruitlessly for aid,
Their parchèd mouths oped eager to the shower
So thin and sleety in that arctic clime,
  Their last hard crust was shared
  Impartial in equality;   90
  And, in the dreadful night

When all had failed, even hope,
　Together they had shared the gleam
　　Shot from yon lighthouse tower
　　Across the waste of waves.　　　　　　　　　95
And therefore are they brave, free, generous,—
For who that had so long fought hand to hand
With famine, toil and hazard, smiled at Death
When, leaning from the bursting billow's height,
He stares so ghastly terrible, would waste　　　　100
One needless word for life's contested toys?
Who that had shared his last and nauseous crust
With Famine and a friend would not divide
A landsman's meal with one who needed it?
Who that could rule the elements and spurn　　　105
Their fiercest rage would bow before a slave
Decked in the fleetingness of earthly power?
Who that had seen the soul of Nature work,
Blind, changeless, and eternal in her paths,
Would shut his eyes and ears, quaking before　　110
The bubble of a Bigot's blasphemy?[1]

　　The faintly moving prow
Divided Ocean's smoothness languidly.
　　A landsman there reclined,
　With lowering, close-contracted brow,　　　　115
　And mouth updrawn at intervals
As fearful of his fluctuating bent,
　　His eyes wide-wandering round

---

[1] It is remarkable that few are more experimentally convinced of the doctrine of Necessity than old sailors, who have seen much and various service. The peculiarly engaging and frank generosity of seafaring men probably is an effect of this cause. Those employed in small and ill-equipped trading-vessels seem to possess this generosity in a purer degree than those of a King's ship. The habit of subjection and coercion imbued into the latter may suffice to explain the cause of the difference. [*Shelley's footnote.*]

111 blasphemy?[1] *conjectural reference for Shelley's Note, written at the foot of the pages covering 95–127*

In insecure malignity,
Rapacious, mean, cruel and cowardly,   120
Casting upon the loveliness of day
    The murkiness of villainy.
By other nurses than the battling storm,
Friendship, Equality and Sufferance,
        His manhood had been cradled,—   125
Inheritor to all the vice and fear
Which kings and laws and priests and conquerors spread
        On the woe-fertilized world.
        Yes, in the dawn of life,
When guileless confidence and unthinking love   130
        Dilate all hearts but those
Which servitude or power has cased in steel,
He bound himself to an unhappy woman,
Not of those pure and heavenly links that Love
        Twines round a feeling to Freedom dear,   135
But of vile gold, cank'ring the breast it binds,
        Corroding and inflaming every thought,
        Till vain desire, remorse and fear
        Envenom all the being.
Yet did this chain, though rankling in the soul   140
Not bind the grosser body; he was wont
        All means to try of thriving;
To those above him the most servile cringe
That ignorance e'er gave to titled Vice
        Was simperingly yielded;   145
To those beneath the frown which Commerce darts
On cast-off friends unprofitably poor
        Was less severe than his.

        There was another too,—
        One of another mould   150
He had been cradled in the wildest storm
        Of Passion and, though now
The feebler light of worn-out energies

Shone on his soul, yet ever and anon
    A flash of tempests long passed by   155
      Would wake to pristine visions.
Now he was wrapt in a wild, woeful dream—
    Deeply his soul could love—
And, as he gazèd on the boundless sea
Chequered with sunbeams and with shade   160
Alternate to infinity,
    He fell into a dream.

    He dreamed that all he loved
Across the shoreless wastes were voyaging
By that unpitying landsman piloted,   165
    And that at length they came
    To a black and sullen island rock.
    Barren the isle—no egg,
Which sea-mews leave upon the wildest shore;
    Barren the isle—no blade   170
Of grass, no seaweed, not the vilest thing
    For human nutriment.

He struggled with the pitiless landsman there
    But, nerved though his frame with love,
    Quenchless, despairing love,   175
    It nought availed; strong Power
    Truth, love and courage vanquished;
A rock was piled upon his feeble breast,—
    All was subdued but that
Which is immortal, unsubduable.   180

    He still continued dreaming;
    The rock upon his bosom quenched not
The frenzy and defiance of his eye.
But the strong and coward landsman laughed to scorn

---

167 ⟨sullen⟩ *over* barren *written, apparently, in anticipation of 168, 170.*
Despite smudging the last three letters seem dear.

His unprevailing fortitude,   185
And, in security of malice, stabbed
One who accompanied his voyagings.
    The blood gushed forth, the eye grew dim,
    The nerve relaxed, the life was gone;
    His smile of dastardly revenge   190
      Glared upon [the] dead frame;
    Then back the victim flung his head;
    In horror insupportable,
Upon the jagged rock whereon he lay,—
    And human nature paused awhile   195
    In pity to his woe.

    When he awaked to life
She whom he loved was bending over him,
    Haggard her sunken eye,
    Bloodless her quivering lips.—   200
    She bended to bestow
The burning moisture from her feverish tongue
    To lengthen out his life
    Perhaps till succour came!—
But more her dear soft eyes in languid love,   205
When life's last gleam was flickering in decay,
    The waning spark rekindled,
And the faint lingering kiss of her withered lips
Mingled a rapture with his misery.
    A bleeding sister lay   210
    Beside this wretched pair
And he, the dastard of relentless soul,
In moody malice lowered over all.

    And this is but a dream!
    For yonder—see! The port in sight   215
    The vessel makes towards it!
    The sight of their safety then,
    And the hum of the populous town,

Awakened them from a night of horror
  To a day of secure delights.   220

    Lo! here, a populous town;
  Two dark rocks either side defend,
  The quiet water sleeps within,
Reflecting every roof and every mast.
    A populous town?—It is a den   225
Where wolves keep lambs to fatten on their blood,—
'Tis a distempered spot: should there be one
Just, dauntless, rational, he would appear
    A madman to the rest.
Yes! smooth-faced tyrants, chartered by a Power   230
Called King, who in the castellated keep
Of a far-distant land wears out his days
Of miserable dotage, pace the quay,
And by the magic of that dreadful word,
Hated though dreadful, shield their impotence,   235
Their lies, their murders and their robberies.
See, where the sailor, absent many years,
With Heaven in his rapture-speaking eyes,
Seeks the low cot where all his wealth reposes,
To bring himself for joy and his small store,   240
Hard-earned by years of peril and of toil,
For comfort to his famine-wasted babes.
Deep in the dark blue sea the unmoving moon
Gleams beautifully quiet,—such a night
When the last kiss from Mary's quivering lips   245
Unmanned him. To the well-known door he speeds;
His faint hand pauses on the latch.—His heart
Beats eagerly,—when suddenly the gang
Dissolves his dream of rapture. No delay!
No pity!—Unexpostulating Power   250
Deals not in human feelings. He is stript
By those low slaves whose masters' names inflict

252 masters'] masters *Esd.*

Curses more fell than even themselves would give!
The Indian muslins and the Chinese toys
(These for small gain and those for boundless love   255
Thus carefully concealed) are torn away,—
The very handkerchief his Mary gave,
Which in unchanging faithfulness he wore,
Rent from his manly neck! His kindling eye
Beamed vengeance, and the tyrants' manacles   260
Shook on his struggling arm: 'Where is my wife?
'Where are my children?' Close beside him stood
A sleek and pampered townsman: 'Oh! your wife
'Died last year in the House of Industry;
'Your young ones all are dead, except one brat   265
'Stubborn as you—parish apprentice now.'

They have appropriated human life
And human happiness,—but these weigh nought
In the nice-balanced Politician's scale,
Who finds that murder is expedient,   270
And that vile means can answer glorious ends.
Wide Nature has outstretched her fertile earth
In commonage to all,—but they have torn
Her dearest offspring from her bleeding breast,
Have disunited liberty and life,   275
Severed all right from duty, and confused
Virtue with selfishness,—the grass-green hills
The fertile valleys and the limpid streams,
The beach on the sea-shore, the sea itself,
The very snow-clad mountain-peaks, whose height   280
Forbids all human footstep, the ravines,
Where cataracts have roared ere Monarchs were,—
Nature, fair Earth, and Heaven's untainted air
Are all apportioned out.—Some bloated Lord,
Some priestly pilferer or some Snake of Law,   285
Some miserable mockery of a man,

264 last year] this time year *Esd*.

Some slave without a heart looks over these
And calls them *Mine*, in self-approving pride!
The millionth of the produce of the vale
He sets apart for *charity*. Vain fool!   290
He gives in mercy, while stern Justice cries:
'Be thou as one of them,—resign thine hall
'Brilliant with murder's trophies, and the board
'Loaded with surfeiting viands, and the gems
'Which millions toil to buy thee.—Get thee hence   295
'And dub thyself a man,—then dare to throw
'One act of usefulness, one thought of love
'Into the balance of thy past misdeeds!'

33

A DIALOGUE

1809

DEATH

Yes! my dagger is drenched with the blood of the brave,
I have sped with Love's wings from the battlefield grave,
    Where Ambition is hushed 'neath the peace-giving sod,
    And slaves cease to tremble at Tyranny's nod;
I offer a calm habitation to thee,—   5
Victim of grief, wilt thou slumber with me?
    Drear and damp is my hall, but a mild Judge is there,
    Who steeps in oblivion the brands of Despair;
Nor a groan of regret, nor a sigh, nor a breath
Dares dispute with grim Silence the empire of Death,   10

TITLE: *Esd.* AUTOGRAPH: *Esd. Hogg MS., now lost.* TEXT: *Esd.* DATE: *Esd.,*
PRINTED: *Hogg, from MS, now lost,* Life, *1858. From a transcript of Esd.,
Ingpen & Peck,* Jul. *1927, but see below and Intr.* § *8.*
  1 Yes *Esd.*] For *1858*   drenched with *Esd.*] bathed in *1858*   2 battlefield
Esd.] battlefield's *1927*   I come, care-worn tenant of life, from the grave *1858*
3 Ambition is hushed *Esd.*] Innocence sleeps *1858*   4 slaves *Esd.*] the good
1858   6 Victim *Esd.*] Say, victim *1858*   7 My mansion is damp, cold
silence is there, *1858*   8 But it lulls in oblivion the fiends of despair, *1858*
9 Nor . . . nor . . . nor *Esd.*] not . . . not . . . not *1858*

Nor the howlings of envy resound through the gloom
That shrouds in its mantle the slaves of the tomb;
I offer a calm habitation to thee,—
Say, victim of grief, wilt thou slumber with me?

MORTAL

Mine eyelids are heavy, my soul seeks repose,   15
It longs in thy arms to embosom its woes,
   It longs in that realm to deposit its load,
   Where no longer the scorpions of Perfidy goad,—
Where the phantoms of Prejudice vanish away,
And Bigotry's bloodhounds lose scent of their prey;   20
   Yet tell me, dark Death: when thine empire is o'er,
   What awaits on Futurity's mist-circled shore?

DEATH

Cease, cease, wayward Mortal! I dare not unveil
The shadows that float o'er Eternity's vale;
   What think'st thou will wait thee? A Spirit of Love[1]   25
   That will hail thy blest advent to mansions above;
For Love, Mortal, gleams through the gloom of my sway,
And the clouds that surround me fly fast at its ray.

[1] The author begs to be understood by this expression neither to mean the Creator of the Universe nor the Christian Deity. When this little poem was written the line stood thus: 'What waits for the good?' but he has altered it on transcription because, however his feelings may love to linger on a future state of happiness, neither justice, reason nor passion can reconcile to his belief that the crimes of this life, equally necessary and inevitable as its virtues, should be punished in another.

>   . . . earth in itself
>   Contains at once the evil and the cure;
>   And all-sufficing Nature can chastise
>   Those who transgress her law . . .

[*Shelley's footnote.*]

11–12 *not in 1858*   16 arms *Esd.*] cells *1858*   17 that realm *Esd.*] thy cells *1858*   22 mist-circled *Esd.*] mist-covered *Esd., 1927*   24 o'er *Esd.*] on *1858*   25 What think'st thou will wait thee? *Esd.*] Nought waits for the good but *1858*   26 thy *Esd.*] their *1858*   mansions *Esd.*] regions *1858*   28 And the clouds that *Esd.*] And the shades which *1858*

Hast thou *loved*?—Then depart from these regions of hate,
And in slumber with me quench the arrows of fate, 30
That canker and burn in the wounds of a heart
That urges its sorrows with me to depart;
I offer a calm habitation to thee,—
Say, victim of grief, wilt thou slumber with me?

MORTAL

Oh, sweet is thy slumber! and sweeter the ray 35
Which after thy night introduces the day;
How soft, how persuasive, self-interest's breath,
Though it floats to mine ear from the bosom of Death!
I hoped that I quite was forgotten by all,
Yet a lingering friend may be grieved at my fall, 40
And Virtue forbids, though I languish, to die,
When departure might heave Virtue's breast with a sigh.
Yet, Death!—oh, my friend! snatch this form to thy shrine,
And I fear, dear destroyer, I shall not repine.

34

[EYES]

1810

How eloquent are eyes!
Not the rapt Poet's frenzied lay
When the soul's wildest feelings stray
Can speak so well as they.

∧ 29 *loved? Esd.*] loved? *1858*   30 quench *Esd.*] blunt *1858*   31–32
not in 1858 or 1927   35 sweeter *Esd.*] sweet is *1858*   37 soft *Esd.*]
concealed *1858*   40 may *Esd.*] might *1858*   41 Virtue *Esd.*] duty *1858*
43 Yet *Esd.*] O *1858*

∨ AUTOGRAPH, DATE, TEXT: *Esd.*   PRINTED: *1–13, from a transcript of Esd.*,
Rossetti, PW, *1870* TITLE: *Rossetti, 1870, Ingpen & Peck*, Jul. *1927*.
  2 Poet's *1870*] Poets *Esd.*

How eloquent are eyes!   5
Not music's most impassioned note
On which Love's warmest fervours float
   Like them bids rapture rise.

Love, look thus again!—
That your look may light a waste of years,   10
Darting the beam that conquers cares
   Through the cold shower of tears!
   Love, look thus again!—
That Time the victor, as he flies,
May pause to gaze upon thine eyes,—   15
   A victor then in vain!

Yet no!—Arrest not Time!
For Time, to others dear, we spurn;
When Time shall *be* no more we burn,
   When Love meets full return.   20
   Ah, no!—Arrest not Time!—
Fast let him fly on eagle wing,
Nor pause till Heaven's unfading spring
   Breathes round its holy clime.

   Yet quench that thrilling gaze   25
Which passionate Friendship arms with fire!
For what will eloquent eyes inspire
   But feverish, false desire?
   Quench then that thrilling gaze!—
For age may freeze the tremulous joy,   30
But age can never *love* destroy,—
   It lives to better days.

   Age cannot love destroy!—
Can perfidy then blight its flower,
Even when, in most unwary hour,   35
   It blooms in Fancy's bower?

8 Like them *1870*] Like they *Esd.* bids *1870*] bid *Esd.*

Age cannot love destroy!—
Can slighted vows then rend the shrine
On which its chastened splendours shine
Around a dream of joy?   40

35

'HOPES THAT BUD...'

1810

Hopes that bud in youthful breasts
    Live not through the lapse of time;
Love's rose a host of thorns invests,
    And ungenial is the clime
      Where its blossoms blow.   5
Youth says, 'The purple flowers are mine,'
    That fade the while they glow.

Dear the boon to Fancy given,
    Retracted while 'tis granted;
Sweet the rose that breathes in Heaven,   10
    Although on Earth 'tis planted
      Where its blossoms blow,
Where by the frosts its leaves are riven
    That fade the while they glow.

AUTOGRAPH: *Esd. Pf.*   TEXT, DATE: *Esd.*   PRINTED: *1–14, from Pf., Hogg,* Life, *1858; 1–14, from a transcript of Esd., Ingpen & Peck,* Jul. *1927. See below, and* Intr. § *8.*

  1 bud *Esd.*] swell *Pf.*   2 not through *Esd.*] they thro *Pf.* they this *1858* lapse *Esd.*] waste *Pf., 1927*   3 a *Esd.*] an *Pf.*   invests *Pf.*] invest *Esd.* 4 And *Esd.*] Cold *Pf.*   5 Blossoms *Esd.*] honours *Pf.*   6–7 *alternatively* mine . . . glow'   7 That fade *Esd.*] Which die *Pf.*   9 while 'tis *Esd.*] whilst it's *Pf.*   10 that breathes *Esd.*] which lives *Pf.*   11 planted *Pf.*] planten *Esd.*   12 blossoms *Esd.*] honours *Pf., 1927*

The pure soul lives that heart within   15
    Which age cannot remove
If undefiled by tainting sin,—
    A sanctuary of love,
      Where its blossoms blow,—
Where, in this unsullied shrine,   20
    They fade not while they glow.

36

TO THE MOONBEAM

23 September 1809

Moonbeam, leave the shadowy dale,
    To cool this burning brow!
Moonbeam, why art thou so pale,
As thou glidest along the midnight vale,
    Where dewy flowrets grow?   5
      Is it to mimic me?
      Ah, that can never be;
      For thy path is bright,
      And the clouds are light,
That at intervals shadow the star-studded night.   10

In place of 15–20, following a row of crosses, Pf. has
    Age cannot love destroy
      But perfidy can blast the flower
      E'en when in most unwary hour
      It blooms in Fancy's bower
    Age cannot love destroy
      But Perfidy can rend the shrine
      In which its vermeil splendors shine
See n.

AUTOGRAPH: *Esd. Pf.*   TITLE: *Pf.*   DATE, TEXT: *Esd.*   PRINTED: *From Pf.*
Hogg, Life, 1858. From a transcript of Esd., Ingpen & Peck, Jul. 1927. See
below and Intr. § *8.*
  1 dale *Esd.*] vale *Pf.*   2 cool *Esd.*] bathe *Pf.*   3 Moonbeam *Esd.,*
Pf.] Moonbeam cool *1927*   4 As thou walkest oer the dewy dale *Pf.*   5
dewy flowrets *Esd.*] humble wild flowers *Pf.*   7 Ah *Esd.*] But *Pf.*   8
thy path *Esd.*] Thine orb *Pf.*

Now all is deathy still on earth;
Nature's tired frame reposes;
Yet, ere the golden morning's birth
Its radiant gates uncloses,
Flies forth her balmy breath.   15
But mine is the midnight of death,
And Nature's morn
To my bosom forlorn
Brings but a gloomier night, implants a deadlier thorn.

Wretch, suppress the glare of madness   20
Struggling in thine haggard eye!
For the keenest throb of sadness,
Pale despair's most sickening sigh,
Is but to mimic me.
But that can never be,   25
When the darkness of care
And the death of despair
Seem in my breast but joys to the pangs that rankle
there.

37–40

[FOUR POEMS TO MARY]

November 1810

[SHELLEY'S] ADVERTISEMENT

The few poems immediately following are selected from many written during
three weeks of an entrancement caused by hearing Mary's story. I hope that
the delicate and discriminating genius of the friend who related it to me will
allow the publication of the heart-breaking facts under the title of 'Leonora'.

∧ 13 Yet *over* And ere *Esd.*] And ere *Pf.* Yet in *1927*   14 gates *Esd.*] hues
Pf., 1927   15 her *Esd.*] its *Pf.*   25 But that can never be *Esd.*] And
this must ever be *Pf.*   26 darkness *Esd.*] twilight *Pf.*   27 death *Esd.*]
night *Pf.*   28 rankle *Esd.*] walk *Pf.* wake *1858*

∨ TITLES: *See n.*   DATE: *Esd. (with no. 37)*   AUTOGRAPH, TEXT: *Esd.*

For myself, at that time, 'nondum amabam, et amare amabam, quaerebam quid amarem, amans amare'.

Mary died three months before I heard her tale.

37

TO MARY I

Dear girl, thou art wildered by madness!
    Yet do not look so, sweet,—
I could share in the sigh of thy sadness;
    Thy woe my soul could meet.

I loved a heart sincerely,   5
    Yes, dear it was to mine—
Yet, Mary, I love more dearly
    One tender look of thine.

Oh, do not say that Heaven
    Will frown on errors past,—   10
Thy faults are all forgiven,
    Thy virtues ever last.[1]

The cup with death o'erflowing
    I'll drink, fair girl, to thee;
For when the storm is blowing   15
    To shelter we may flee.

[1] This opinion is, of all others, the most deeply rooted in my conviction. The enquirer will laugh at it as a dream, the Christian will abhor it as a blasphemy—Mary who repeatedly attempted suicide, yet was unwilling to die alone.—Nor is it probable that she would, had I instead of my friend been subjected to the trial of sitting a summer's night by her side, whilst two glasses of poison stood on the table and she folded me to her tremulous bosom in ecstasies of friendship and despair! [*Shelley's footnote.*]

12 *conjectural reference for Shelley's note, written at the foot of pages covering 7–28 and extending to the next page.*

SHELLEY'S FOOTNOTE.—*Cancelled at end:* What are the Romances of Leadenhall Str. to this of real life?

Thou canst not bear to languish
   In this frail chain of clay,
And I am tired of anguish,—
   Love, let us haste away!   20

Like thee I fear to weather
   Death's darksome wave alone,—
We'll take the voyage together,
   Come, Mary, let's begone!

Strange mists my woe efface, love,   25
   And thou art pale in Death,—
Give one, one last embrace, love,
   And we resign our breath.

38

TO MARY II

Fair one, calm that bursting heart!
   Dares then fate to frown on thee,
Lovely, spotless as thou art—
   Though its worst poison lights on me?
      Then dry that tear,—   5
      Thou needest not fear
These woes when thy limbs are cold on the bier.

Start not from winter's breathing, dearest,
   Though bleak is yonder hill,—
As perjured love the blast thou fearest   10
   Is not half so deadly chill!
      Like these winds that blow
      No remorse does it know
And colder it strikes than the driving snow.

The tomb is damp and dark and low,   15
 Yet with thee the tomb I do not dread,—
There is not a place of frightful woe
 Where with thee I'd refuse to lay my head.
  But our souls shall not sleep
  In the grave damp and deep   20
But in love and devotion[1] their holy-day keep.

39

TO MARY III

Mary, Mary, art thou gone
 To sleep in thine earthy cell?
Presses thy breast the death-cold stone,
Pours none the tear, the sob, the groan,
Where murdered virtue sleeps alone,   5
 Where its first glory fell?

Mary, Mary, past is past!
 I submit in silence to fate's decree,
Though the tear of distraction gushes fast
And, at night when the lank reeds hiss in the blast,   10
 My spirit mourns in sympathy.

Thou wert more fair in mind than are
 The fabled heavenly train,
But thine was the pang of corroding care,
Thine cold contempt and lone despair,   15
And thwarted love, more hard to bear.
And I, wretch, weep that such they were,
 And I—still drag my chain.

---

[1] The expression *devotion* is not used in a religious sense; for which abuse of this lovely word few have a greater horror than the Author. [*Shelley's footnote.*]

Thou wert but born to weep, to die,
To feel dissolved the dearest tie,   20
    Its fragments by the pitiless world
    Adown the blast of fortune hurled,
To strive with envy's wreckful storm,—
    Thou wert but born to weep and die,
    Nor could thy ceaseless misery   25
      Nor heavenly virtues aught avail,
      Nor taintless innocence prevail
With the world's slaves thy love to spare,
Nor the magic, unearthly atmosphere
That wrapt thine ethereal form.   30

    Such, loveliest Mary, was thy fate,
      And such is Virtue's doom:
    Contempt, neglect and hatred wait,
    Where yawns a wide and dreary gate,
      To drag its votaries to the tomb,—   35
Sweet flower, that blooms amid the weeds
    Where the rank serpent Interest feeds!

40

TO THE LOVER OF MARY

Drink the exhaustless moonbeam, where its glare
    Wanly lights murdered virtue's funeral
    And tremulous sheds on the corpse-shrouding pall
      A languid, languid flare!—
Hide thee, poor wretch, where yonder baleful yew   5
    Sheds o'er the clay that now is tenantless,
    Whose spirit once thrilled to thy warm caress,
      Its deadly, deadly dew!
The moonray will not quench thy misery,

30 ethereal] etherial *over* heavenly *in Esd.*

But the yew's death-drops will bring peace to thee,   10
And yonder clay-cold grave thy bridal bed shall be.

And since the spirit dear that breathes of Heaven
  Has burst the powerless bondage of its clay
  And soars an angel to eternal day,
    Purged of its earthly leaven,   15
Thy yearnings now shall bend thee to the tomb,
  Oblivion blot a life without a stain,
  And death's cold hand round thy heart's ceaseless pain
    Enfold its veil of gloom.
The wounds shall close of Misery's scorpion goad   20
When Mary greets thee in her blest abode
And worships holy Love in purity, thy God.

Oh, this were joy, and such as none would fear
  To purchase by a life of passing woe!—
  For on this earth the sickly flowers that glow   25
    Breathe of perfection there.
Yet live,—for others barter thine own bliss,
  And living show what towering virtue dares
  To accomplish even in this vale of tears!
    Turn Hell to Paradise   30
And, spurning selfish joy, soar high above
The Heaven of Heavens, let even eternal Love,
Despised awhile, thy sense of holier Virtue[1] prove!

[1] As if they were not synonymous! [*Shelley's footnote.*]

[BIGOTRY'S VICTIM]

1810

Dares the llama, most fleet of the sons of the wind,
    The lion to rouse from his lair?
When the tiger awakes can the fast-fleeting hind
    Repose trust in his footsteps of air?
No! abandoned it sinks in helpless despair,   5
    The monster transfixes his prey,
    On the sand flows its life-blood away;
And the rocks and the woods to the death-yells reply,
Protracting the horrible harmony.

Yet the fowl of the desert, when danger encroaches,   10
    Dares dreadless to perish, defending her brood,
Though the fiercest of cloud-piercing tyrants approaches,
    Thirsting—aye, thirsting for blood,
    And demands, like mankind, his brother for food;
        Yet more lenient, more gentle than they;   15
        For hunger, not glory, the prey
Must perish. Revenge does not howl o'er the dead,
Nor ambition with fame bind the murderer's head.

Though weak as the llama that bounds on the mountains,
    And endued not with fast-fleeting footsteps of air,   20
Yet, yet will I draw from the purest of fountains,
    Though a fiercer than tigers is there.

TITLE: *See Intr. § 6.*   DATE: *Esd.*   AUTOGRAPH: *Esd. TCU*   TEXT:
Esd.   PRINTED: *From TCU, Hogg,* Life, *1858. From a transcript of Esd., Ingpen & Peck, Jul. 1927. See below and Intr. § 8.*
    2 lair *Esd.*] scull covered lair *TCU*   3 awakes *Esd., TCU*] approaches *1858*   5 it *Esd.*] he *TCU*   helpless despair *Esd.*] a trance of despair *TCU* 7 its *Esd.*] his *TCU, 1927*   8 And the rocks and the woods *Esd.*] Whilst India's rocks *TCU*   the *Esd.*] his *TCU*   10 desert *TCU*] desart *Esd. See n.*   11 dreadless *Esd.*] fearless *TCU*   16 hunger *Esd.*] hunger *italicized TCU*   17 o'er *Esd.*] in *TCU*   18 bind *Esd.*] crown *TCU*

Though, more frightful than death, it scatters despair,
 And its shadow, eclipsing the day,
 Spreads the darkness of deepest dismay   25
On the withered and withering nations around,
And the war-mangled corpses that rot on the ground.

They came to the fountain to draw from its stream
 Waves too poisonously lovely for mortals to see;
They basked for a while in the love-darting beam, 30
 Then perished,—and perished like me.
For in vain from the grasp of Religion I flee;
 The most tenderly loved of my soul
 Are slaves to its chilling control.
It pursues me, it blasts me! Oh, where shall I fly? 35
What remains but to curse it, to curse it and die?

42

[LOVE AND TYRANNY]

1809

I will kneel at thine altar, will crown thee with bays,
 Whether God, Love or Virtue thou art!
Thou shalt live,—aye, more long than these perishing lays:
 Thou shalt live in this high-beating heart!
Dear Love! from its life-springs thou never shalt part, 5

⋀ 23 frightful *Esd.*] dreadful *TCU* 24 And *Esd.*] Tho *TCU* eclipsing *Esd.*]
eclipses *TCU* 25 Spreads *Esd.*] And *TCU* 26 Spreads the influence of
soul-chilling terror around *TCU* 27 war-mangled *Esd.*] lowers on the *TCU*
29 poisonously lovely *Esd*]. pure too celestial *TCU* 30 basked *Esd.*] bathed
TCU the *Esd.*] its *TCU, 1927* love-darting *Esd.*] silvery *TCU* 32 Religion
Esd., TCU] the Bigot *1858* 34 its *Esd., TCU*] his *1858* chilling *Esd.*]
hated *TCU* 35 It . . . it *Esd., TCU*] He . . . he *1858* Oh, where shall
Esd., TCU] 'Tis vain that *1858* 36 it . . . it *Esd., TCU*] him . . . him *1858*

⋀ AUTOGRAPH, TEXT, DATE: *Esd.* TITLE: *See Intr. § 6.*
 5 shalt] shall *Esd.*

Though Prejudice, clanking her chain,
Though Interest, groaning in gain,
May tell me thou closest to Heaven the door,
May tell me that thine is the way to be poor.

The victim of merciless tyranny's power   10
  May smile at his chains if with thee;
The most sense-enslaved loiterer in Passion's sweet bower
  Is a wretch if unhallowed by thee;
Thine, thine is the bond that alone binds the free,—
    Can the free worship bondage? Nay more,   15
    What they feel not, believe not? Adore
What, if felt, if believed, if existing, must give
To thee to create, to eternize, to live?—

For Religion, more keen than the blasts of the North,
  Darts its frost through the self-palsied soul;   20
Its slaves on the work of destruction go forth,—
  The divinest emotions that roll
Submit to the rod of its impious control;
    At the venomous blast of its breath
    Love, concord, lies gasping in death,   25
Philanthropy utters a war-drownèd cry,
And selfishness conquering cries 'Victory'!

Can we then, thus tame, thus impassive, behold
  That alone whence our life springs destroyed?
Shall Prejudice, Priestcraft, Opinion and Gold,   30
  Every Passion with interest alloyed,
Where Love ought to reign, fill the desolate void?
    But the Avenger arises, the throne
    Of selfishness totters,—its groan
Shakes the nations—it falls, Love seizes the sway;   35
The sceptre it bears unresisted away.

43

FRAGMENT OF A POEM, &c.—

[See Appendix]

44

ON AN ICICLE THAT CLUNG TO THE GRASS
OF A GRAVE

1809

Oh! take the pure gem to where southernly breezes
   Waft repose to some bosom as faithful as fair,
In which the warm current of love never freezes,
   As it circulates freely and shamelessly there,
     Which, untainted by crime, unpolluted by care,   5
Might dissolve this dim icedrop, might bid it arise,
Too pure for these regions, to gleam in the skies.

For I found the pure gem, when the daybeam returning,
   Ineffectual gleams on the snow-spangled plain,
When to others the longed-for arrival of morning   10

AUTOGRAPH: *Esd. Pf.* TITLE, DATE, TEXT: *Esd.* PRINTED: *From Pf., Hogg,*
Life, 1858. From a transcript of Esd., Ingpen & Peck, Jul. 1927, but see below
and Intr. § 8.
   1 southernly *Esd., Pf.*] southerly *1858, 1927*   4 As it circulates *Esd.*] As
it rises *Pf.* Circulates *1927*   freely and shamelessly *Esd.*] unmingled with
selfishness *Pf.*   5 crime *Esd.*] Pride *Pf.*   6 this *Esd., Pf.*] the *1927*
Between 7 and 8 Pf. has this stanza
            Or where the stern warrior his country defending
              Dares fearless the dark-rolling battle to pour
            Or o'er the fell corpse of a dread Tyrant bending
              Where Patriotism red with his guilt-reeking gore
              Plants Liberty's flag on the slave-peopled shore,
            With Victory's cry, with the shout of the free,
            Let it fly taintless Spirit to mingle with thee.

9 snow-spangled *Esd.*] snow-covered *Pf.*   10 longed-for *Esd.*] wished for
Pf.

Brings relief to long night-dreams of soul-racking pain;
But regret is an insult—to grieve is in vain:
And why should we grieve that a spirit so fair
Sought Heaven to meet with its kindred there?

Yet 'twas some angel of kindness, descending   15
   To share in the load of mortality's woe,
Who, over thy lowly-built sepulchre bending,
   Bade sympathy's tenderest teardrops to flow,
   And consigned the rich gift to the sister of snow;
And if angels can weep, sure I may repine,   20
And shed teardrops, though frozen to ice, on thy shrine.

45

'COLD ARE THE BLASTS...'

[See Appendix]

11 night-dreams *Esd.*] visions *Pf.*   13 And *Esd.*] Say *above* And *under-lined Pf.*   14 Sought *Esd.*] Seeks *Pf.*   meet *Esd.*] mix *Pf.*   its *Esd.*] its own *1858, 1927*   15 Yet *Esd.*] But still *Pf.*   angel *Esd.*] spirit *Pf.*   18 teardrops *Esd.*] tear drop *Pf.*   19 Not for *thee* soft compassion celestials did know *Pf.*   20 And *Esd.*] But *Pf.*   angels *Esd.*] angels *italicized Pf.*, *1927*   I *Esd.*] Man *italicized Pf.*   21 May weep in mute grief o'er thy low-laid shrine. *Pf.*

After 21 Pf. has this stanza
   And did I then say for the Altar of Glory
     That the earliest the loveliest flowers I'd entwine
   Tho' with millions of blood-reeking victims 'tis gory
     Tho' the tears of the widow polluted its shine
     Tho' around it the orphans, the fatherless pine.
   Oh! fame all thy glories I'd yield for a tear
   To shed on the grave of an heart so sincere.

HENRY AND LOUISA[1]
1809

A POEM IN TWO PARTS

She died for love—and he for glory

PART THE FIRST

The Parting

Scene: England

I

Where are the heroes? Sunk in death they lie.
  What toiled they for? Titles and wealth and fame.
But the wide heaven is now their canopy,
    And 'legal murderers' their loftiest name.
    Enshrined on brass their glory and their shame   5
What though torn Peace and martyred Freedom see?—
What though to most remote posterity
    Their names, their selfishness, for aye enscrolled,
    A shuddering world's blood-boltered eyes behold,
Mocking mankind's unbettered misery?—   10
    Can this perfection give? Can valour prove
    One wish for others' bliss, one throb of love? . . .

---

[1] The stanza of this poem is radically that of Spenser although I suffered myself at the time of writing it to be led into occasional deviations. These defects I do not alter now, being unwilling to offer any outrage to the living portraiture of my own mind, bad as it may be pronounced. [*Shelley's footnote.*]

TITLE, DATE, AUTOGRAPH, TEXT: *Esd.*
  3 canopy *over* canopies

II

Yet darest thou boast thyself superior thou,
   Vile worm, whom lovely woman deigns to bless?—
And, meanly selfish, bask in glory's glow,   15
    Rending the soul-spun ties of tenderness
    Where all desires rise for thine happiness?
Canst thou boast thus and hope to be forgiven?
   Oh, when thou started'st from her last caress,
From purest love by vulgar glory driven,   20
Couldst thou have e'er deserved, if thou resigned'st, Heaven?

III

IV

21 *the stanza-headings III, IV, and V are followed in Esd. by blank spaces down to the line here numbered as 22. See n.*

V

⟨And, shadowed by Affection's purple wing,
Bid thee forget how Time's fast footstep sped:
Would die in peace when thou wert mingled with the dead.⟩

VI

Had glory's fire consumed each tender tie   25
    That links to love the heaven-aspiring soul?
Could not that voice, quivering in agony,
    That struggling pale resolve, that dared control
Passion's wild flood when wildest it did roll,—
Could not impassioned tenderness that burst   30
    Cold prudery's bondage, owning all it felt,—
Could not these, warrior, quench thy battle-thirst?
    Nought this availed thine iron-bound breast to melt,—
    To make thy footsteps pause where love and freedom dwelt?

VII

Yes, every soul-nerve vibrated. A space   35
    Enchained in speechless awe the warrior stood;
Superior reason, virtue, manner, grace
    Claimed for a space their rights,—in varying mood
    Before her lovely eyes in thought he stood,
Whilst glory's train flashed on his mental eye,   40
    Which wandered wildly where the fight's red flood,
The crash of death, the storm of victory
Roll round the hopes of love that only breathe to die.

VIII

Then she exclaimed, as love-nerved sense returned,
  'Go!—Mingle in thy country's battle-tide! 45
Forget that love's pale torch hath ever burned
  Until thou meet'st me clothed in victor-pride;
May guardian spirits keep thee! Far and wide
O'er the red regions of the day-scorched zone
  For glory seek!—But here thou wilt abide 50
Here in this breast thou wilt abide alone,—
I will thine empire be. My heart shall be thy throne.'

IX

When princes at fair Reason's bidding bend,
  Resigning power for virtue's fadeless meed,
Or spirits of Heaven to man submission lend, 55
  The debt of gratitude is great indeed;
In vain the heart its thankfulness to prove
  Aye might attempt to do the debt away.
Yet what is this compared to Woman's love,—
  Dear Woman's love, the dawn of Virtue's day,— 60
The bliss-inspiring beam, the soul-illuming ray?

X

Then Henry spoke, as he checked the rising tear:
  'That I have loved thee, and must love for ever,
Heaven is a witness—Heaven to whom are dear
  The hearts that earthly chances cannot sever, 65
  Where bloom the flowers that cease to blossom never.
Religion sanctifies the cause: I go
  To execute its vengeance. Heaven will give
To me (so whispers hope) to quell the foe:
  Heaven gives the good to conquer and to live, 70
And thou shalt next to God his votive heart receive.

52 My heart *possibly, in error* thy heart

XI

'Say, is not he the Tyrant of the World.
   And are not we the injured and the brave?
Unmoved shall we behold his flag unfurled,
    Flouting with impious wing Religion's grave,   75
    Triumphant gleaming o'er the passive wave?—
Nor raise an arm nor one short pleasure yield
   The boon of immortality to save?
Hope is our tempered lance, faith is our shield;
Conquest or death for these wait on the gory field.   80

XII

'Even at that hour when hostile myriads clash
   And terrible death shakes his resistless dart,
Mingling wild wailings with the battle crash,
    Then thou and Heaven shall share this votive heart;
    When from pale dissolution's grasp I start,   85
(If Heaven so wills) even then will I be thine,
   Nor can the whelming tomb have power to part
From all it loves a heart that loves like mine—
From thee round whom its hopes, its joys, its fears entwine.'

XIII

A sicklier tint crept o'er Louisa's cheek: 90
   'But thou art dearer far to me than all
That fancy's visions feign, or tongue can speak,—
    Yes! May I die, and be that death eternal,
    When other thoughts but thee my soul enthral!
The joys of heaven I prize thee far above: 95
   Thee, dearest, will my soul its saviour call,—
My faith is thine—my faith-gained heaven thy love,
My hell when cruel Fates thee from these arms remove.

XIV

'Farewell.' She spoke. The warrior's war-steeled breast,
  Quivering in feeling's agonised excess,   100
Scarce drew its breath, to sickliness oppressed
    By mingled self-reproach and tenderness;
    He dared not speak, but rushed from her caress,
The sunny glades, the little birds of spring,
    Twittering from every garlanded recess,   105
Returning verdure's joy that seemed to sing,
Whilst Woe with stern hand smote his every mental string.

XV

The fragrant dew-mists from the ivied thorn,
    Whose form o'ershadowed love's most blissful bower,
Where oft would fly the tranquil time of morn,   110
    Or swifter urge its flight dear evening's hour,
    When purple twilight in the east would lower
And the amorous starbeam kiss the loveliest form
    That ever bruised a pleasure-fainting flower,
Whose emanative eyebeam, thrilling warm,   115
Around her sacred presence shed a rapturing charm,—

XVI

Each object so beloved, each varied tone
    Of heavenly feeling that can never die,
Each little throb his heart had ever known
    Impetuous rushed on fainting memory.   120
    Yet not alone for parted ecstasy
To which he now must bid a long adieu
    Started the bitter tear or burst the sigh:
No, all the pangs that, spite concealment, grew
O'er his Louisa's peace, a deeper soul-pang drew.   125

104 glades,] glades; *Esd.*   107 string.] string; *Esd.*   111 hour,] hower
Esd.   116 charm,—] charm; *Esd.*

XVII

The balmy breath of soul-reviving dawn
   That kissed the bosom of the waveless lake,
Scented with spring-flowers o'er the level lawn,
    Struck on his sense, to woe scarce yet awake;
    He felt its still reproach; the upland brake   130
Rustled beneath his war-steed's eager prance;
    Hastening to Egypt's shore his way to take
But swifter hastening to dispel the trance
Of grief, he hurried on, smothering the last sad glance.

XVIII

Sweet flower! in dereliction's solitude   135
   That scatterest perfume to the unheeding gale,
And in the grove's unconscious quietude
    Murmurest (thyself scarce conscious) thy sad tale!—
    Sure it is subject for the Poet's wail
⟨That faint, that one so worthy to be prized   140
    The fairest flower of the loveliest vale,
To withering Glory should be sacrificed,
That hides his hateful form in Virtue's garb disguised.⟩

XIX

Religion, hated cause of all the woe
   That makes the world this wilderness! Thou spring   145
Whence terror, pride, revenge and perfidy flow!—
    The curses which thy pampered minions bring
    On thee shall Virtue's votary fear to fling?
And thou, dear Love,—thy tender ties to sever,
    To drown in shouts thy bliss-fraught murmuring,   150
Ceaseless shall selfish Prejudice endeavour?
Shall she succeed? Oh, no! Whilst I live, never, never!

140–43 *See n.*

XX

For, by the wrongs that flaming deep
    Within this bosom's agony . . .
That dry the source whence others weep,—   155
    I swear that thou shalt die.

PART THE SECOND

The Meeting

Scene: Africa

I

'Tis night.—No planet's brilliance dares to light
    The dim and battle-blushing scenery;
Friends mixed with foes urge unremitting fight
    Beneath war's suffocating canopy,   160
    And, as sulphureous meteors fire the sky,
Fast flash the deathful thunderbolts of war,
    Whilst groans unite in frightful harmony,
And wakened vultures, shrieking from afar,
Scent their half-murdered prey amid the battle's jar.   165

II

⟨Now had the Genius of the South, sublime
    On mighty Atlas' tempest-cinctured throne,
Looked over Afric's desolated clime,
    Deep wept at slavery's everlasting moan
    And his most dear-belovèd nation's groan   170
The Boreal whirlwind's shadowy wings that sweep
    The varied bosom of the northern world
That hears contending thunders on the deep
    Sees hostile flags on Egypt's strand unfurled,
Brings Egypt's faintest groan to waste and ruin hurled.⟩   175

153 deep *not, I think,* sleep *in Esd.*   154 agony . . .] agony *Esd. See n.*
166–75 *See n.*

III

Is ⟨this⟩ then all that sweeps the midnight sand?
  Tells the wild blast no tales of deeper woe?
Does war alone pollute the unhappy land?
  No,—the low fluttering and the hectic glow
  Of hope, whose sickly flowret scarce can blow,   180
Chilled by the ice-blast of intense despair,
  Anguish that dries the big tear ere it flow,
And maniac love that sits by the beacon's glare,
With eyes on nothing fixed, dim like a mist-clothed star!

IV

No fear save one could daunt her. Ocean's wave,   185
  Bearing Britannia's hired assassins on
To victory's shame or an unhonoured grave,
  Beheld Louisa 'mid an host alone;
  The womanly dress that veiled her fair form is gone,
Gone is the timid wandering of her eye,   190
  Pale firmness nerved her anguished heart to stone:
The sense of shame, the flush of modesty
By stern resolve were quenched or only glowed to die.

V

'Where is my love, my Henry—is he dead?'
  Half drowned in smothered anguish wildly burst   195
From her parched lips—'Is my adored one dead?
  Knows none my Henry? War! thou source accurst
  In whose red flood I see these sands immersed,
Hast thou quite whelmed compassion's tearful spring
  Where thy fierce tide rolls to slake Glory's thirst?   200
Perhaps thou, warrior, some kind word dost bring
From my poor Henry's lips when death its shade did fling.'

---

183 beacon's] beacons *Esd.*   185 her.] her— *Esd.*   187 victory's shame
corrected by Shelley from victory stern,   199 whelmed *above* [dried] *Esd.*

VI

A tear of pity dimmed the warrior's gaze;
　'I know him not, sweet maiden, yet the fight
That casts on Britain's fame a brighter blaze　　　　　205
　　Should spare all yours, if aught I guess aright.
　　But ah! by yonder flash of sulphurous light
The dear-loved work of battle has begun—
　　Fame calls her votaries.' He fled. The night
Had far advanced before the fray was done;　　　　　210
Scarce sunk the roar of war before the rising sun.

VII

But sight of wilder grief where slept the dead
　　Was witnessed by the morn's returning glow,
When frantic o'er the waste Louisa sped
　　　To drink her dying lover's latest vow.　　　　　215
　　　Sighed 'mid her locks the sea-gales as they blew,
Bearing along faint shrieks of dying men,
　　　As if they sympathised with her deep woe;
　Silent she paused a space, and then again
New-nerved by fear and hope, sprang wild across the plain.　220

VIII

See where she stops again!—A ruin's shade
　　Darkens his fading lineaments; his cheek,
On which remorseful pain is deep portrayed,
　　　Glares death-convulsed and ghastly; utterings break,
　　　Shuddering, unformed, his tongue essays to speak.　225
　　　　There low he lies, poor Henry! Where is now
　　　Thy dear, devoted love? Is there no friend
To bathe with tears that anguish-burning brow—
　　　None comfort in this fearful hour to lend,
When to remorseful grief thy parting spirits bend?　　　230

209 begun—] begun. *Esd.*　　　220 fear *possibly* fears *Esd.*　　　226 There
possibly thus　　　227 devoted *possibly* deserted

IX

Yes, pain had steeped each dying limb in flame
  When, mad with mingled hope and pale dismay,
Fleet as the wild deer, his Louisa came,
    Nerved by distraction. A pale tremulous ray
    Flashed on her eyes from the expiring day;   235
Life for a space rushed to his fainting breast,
    The breathing form of love-enlivened clay
In motionless rapture pale Louisa pressed
And, stung by maddening hope, in tears her bliss expressed.

X

Yet was the transport wavering: the dew   240
  Of bodily pain that bathed his pallid brow,
The pangs that through his anguished members flew,
    Though half subdued by Love's returning glow,
    Doubt mixed with lingering hope must needs bestow.
Then she exclaimed, 'Love, I have sought thee far,   245
    Whence our own Albion's milder sea-gales blow
To this stern scene of fame-aspiring war,—
Through waves of danger past thou wert my polar star.

XI

Live then, dear source of life! And let the ray
  Which lights thy kindling eyebeam softly speak   250
That thou hast loved when I was far away.
    Yet thou art pale; death's hectic lights thy cheek!—
    Oh, if one moment Fate the chain should break
Which binds thy soul unchangeably to mine!
    Another moment's pain fate dare not wreak;   255
Another moment—I am ever thine,—
Love, turn those eyes on me! Ah, death has dimmed their
    shine!'

XII

Ceased her voice; the accents mild
   In frightful stillness died away;
More sweet than Memnon's plainings wild   260
    That float upon the morning ray
       Died every sound,—save when,
       At distance o'er the plain,
Britannia's legions, swiftly sweeping
Glory's ensanguined harvest reaping,   265
       Mowed down the field of men,
And the silent ruins, crumbling nigh,
With echoes low prolonged the cry
   Of mingled defeat and victory.

XIII

More low, more faint, yet far more dread   270
   Arose the expiring warrior's groan;
Stretched on the sand, his bloody bed,
In agonised death was Henry laid,
   But he did not fall alone.
Why then that anguished sigh   275
Which seems to tear the vital tie,
   Fiercer than death, more fell
Than tyranny, contempt or hate?
   Why does that breast with horror swell
Which ought to triumph over fate?   280
   Why?—Ask the pallid grief-worn mien
Of poor Louisa, let it speak.
But her firm heart would sooner break
   Than doubt the soul where love had been.

XIV

Now, now he dies!—his parting breath   285
   The sulphurous gust of battle bears;
The shriek, the groan, the gasp of death
   Unmoved Louisa hears,

And a smile of triumph lights her eye
With more than mortal radiancy.— 290
   Sacred to Love a deed is done,
   Gleams through battle-clouds the sun!
Gleams it on all that's good and fair,
Stretched on the earth to moulder there!
     Shall virtue perish? No! 295
   Superior to Religion's tie,
   Emancipate from misery,
Despising self, their souls can know
All the delight love can bestow
   When Glory's phantom fades away 300
   Before Affection's purer ray,—
When tyrants cease to wield the rod,
And slaves to tremble at their nod!

XV

There, near the stunted palms that shroud
   The spot from which their spirits fled, 305
Shall pause the human hounds of blood,
   And own a secret dread;
There shall the victor's steel-clad brow,
Though flushed by conquest's crimson glow,
   Be changed with inward fear; 310
There stern and steady by long command,
The pomp-fed despot's sceptred hand
   Shall shake as if death were near,
Whilst the lone captive in his train
Feels comfort as he shakes his chain. 315

300 When *possibly* Where   311 steady *above* [bronzed]

47

A TRANSLATION OF THE MARSEILLAISE HYMN

c. 19 June 1811

1

Haste to battle, Patriot-Band,
  A day of glory dawns on thee!
Against thy rights is raised an hand,
  The blood-red hand of tyranny!
See, the ferocious slaves of power   5
Across the wasted country scour,
And in thy very arms destroy
The pledges of thy nuptial joy,
  Thine unresisting family!

Chorus

Then citizens form in battle array,
For this is the dawn of a glorious day!—
  March, march, fearless of danger and toil,
  And the rank gore of tyrants shall water your soil!

2

What wills the coward, traitorous train
  Of Kings, whose trade is perfidy?
For whom is forged this hateful chain,
  For whom prepared this slavery?
For you!—On you their vengeance rests,—   5
What transports ought to thrill your breasts!
  Frenchmen! this unhallowed train
  To ancient woe would bind again
    Those souls whom valour has made free!

AUTOGRAPH: *Esd. NYPL (stanza 2 only)* TITLE, TEXT: *Esd.* DATE: *See n.* PRINTED: *A. Koszul in* La Jeunesse de Shelley, *1910, reprinted by Ingpen & Peck, Jul. 1927.*

Chorus

Then citizens etc. . . .

3

What! Shall foreign bands compel
  Us to the laws of tyranny?
Shall hired soldiers hope to quell
  The arm upraised for liberty?
Great God!—By these united arms   5
Shall despots [in] their own alarms
Pass 'neath the yoke made for our head!
Yea, pomp-fed Kings shall quake with dread,
  These masters of Earth's destiny!

Chorus

Then citizens etc. . . .

4

Tremble Kings, despised of Man,
  Ye traitors to your country!
Tremble! Your parricidal plan
  At length shall meet its destiny!
We are all soldiers fit for fight,   5
But if we sink in glory's night
Our Mother Earth will give ye new
The brilliant pathway to pursue
  That leads to death or victory!

Chorus

Then citizens etc. . . .

Stanza 3, line 6 despots in their *Koszul*] despots their *Esd.*

5

Frenchmen! On the guilty brave
  Pour your vengeful energy!—
Yet, in your triumph pitying, save
  The unwilling slaves of tyranny;
But let the gore-stained despots bleed,   5
Be death fell Bouillé's bloodhound-meed,
Chase those unnatural fiends away
Who on their mother's vitals prey
  With more than tiger cruelty!   9

Chorus

Then citizens etc. . . .

6

Sacred Patriotism! Uphold
  The avenging bands who fight with thee!
And thou, more dear than meaner gold,
  Smile on our efforts, Liberty!
Where Conquest's crimson streamers wave   5
Haste thou to the happy brave,
Where at our feet thy dying foes
See, as their failing eyes unclose,
  Our glory and thy victory!   9

Chorus

Then citizens etc. . . .

Stanza 5, line 6 Bouillé's] Bouillie's *Esd.*

WRITTEN IN VERY EARLY YOUTH

? 1807–9

I'll lay me down by the churchyard tree
And resign me to my destiny;
   I'll bathe my brow with the poison dew
   That falls from yonder deadly yew;
And, if it steal my soul away,   5
To bid it wake in realms of day,
   Spring's sweetest flowers shall never be
   So dear to gratitude and me!

Earthborn glory cannot breathe
Within the damp recess of death: 10
   Avarice, Envy, Lust, Revenge
   Suffer there a fearful change,—
All that grandeur ever gave
Moulders in the silent grave;
   Oh, that I slept near yonder yew,   15
   That this tired frame might moulder too!

Yet Pleasure's folly is not mine,
No votarist I at Glory's shrine;
   The sacred gift for which I sigh
Is not to live, to feel alone;   20
   I only ask to calmly die,
That the tomb might melt this heart of stone
   To love beyond the grave.

TITLE, AUTOGRAPH, TEXT: *Esd.*   DATE: *See n.*

ZEINAB AND KATHEMA

Summer 1811

Upon the lonely beach Kathema lay,
  Against his folded arm his heart beat fast;
Through gathering tears the sun's departing ray
  In coldness o'er his shuddering spirit passed,
And, all unfelt, the breeze of evening came   5
That fanned with quivering wing his wan cheek's feeble flame.

'Oh', cried the mourner, 'could this widowed soul
  But fly where yonder sun now speeds to dawn!'
He paused—a thousand thoughts began to roll;
  Like waves they swept in restless tumult on,—   10
Like those fast waves that quick-succeeding beat
Without one lasting shape the beach beneath his feet.

And, now the beamless, broad and yellow sphere
  Half sinking lingered on the crimson sea,
A shape of darksome distance does appear   15
  Within its semi-circled radiancy.
All sense was gone to his betrothèd one—
His eye fell on the form that dimmed the setting sun,—

He thought on his betrothèd. For his youth
  With her that was its charm to ripeness grew;   20
All that was dear in love or fair in truth
  With her was shared as childhood's moments flew,
And mingled with sweet memories of her
Was life's unveiling morn with all its bliss and care.

TITLE, AUTOGRAPH, TEXT: *Esd.*   DATE: *See n.*   PRINTED: *79–84, Dowden,* Life *1886.*
  13–24 *See n.*   13 sea,] sea *Esd.*   16 radiancy.] radiancy *Esd.*
19 betrothèd. For] betrothed . . . for *Esd.*   24 care.] care *Esd.*

A wild and lovely superstition's spell,   25
    Love for the friend that life and freedom gave,
Youth's growing hopes that watch themselves so well,
    Passion so prompt to blight, so strong to save,
And childhood's host of memories combine
Her life and love around his being to entwine.   30

And to their wishes with its joy-mixed pain
    Just as the veil of hope began to fall,
The Christian murderers over-ran the plain
    Ravaging, burning, and polluting all.—
Zeinab was reft to grace the robbers' land;   35
Each drop of kindred blood stained the invaders' brand.

Yes! they had come their holy book to bring,
    Which God's own son's apostles had compiled
That charity and peace and love might spring
    Within a world by God's blind ire defiled.   40
But rapine, war and treachery rushed before
Their hosts, and murder dyed Kathema's bower in gore.

Therefore his soul was widowed, and alone
    He stood in the world's wide and drear expanse;
No human ear could shudder at his groan,   45
    No heart could thrill with his unspeaking glance,—
One only hope yet lingering dared to burn,
Urging to high emprize and deeds that danger spurn.

The glow has failed on Ocean's western line,
    Faded from every moveless cloud above;   50
The moon is up—she that was wont to shine
    And bless thy childish nights of guileless love,
Unhappy one, ere Christian rapine tore
All ties and stained thy hopes in a dear mother's gore.

25 spell,] spell *Esd.*   26 gave,] gave ; *Esd.*   54 dear *possibly* dead

811450   H

The form that in the setting sun was seen   55
    Now in the moonlight slowly nears the shore,
The white sails gleaming o'er the billows green
    That sparkle into foam its prow before,—
A wanderer of the deep it seems to be,
On high adventures bent and feats of chivalry.   60

Then hope and wonder filled the mourner's mind;
    He gazed till vision even began to fail;
When, to the pulses of the evening wind,
    A little boat approaching gave its sail,
Rode on the slow-raised surges near the strand,   65
Ran up the beach and gave some stranger men to land.

'If thou wilt bear me to far England's shore,
    'Thine is this heap—the Christian's God.'
The chief with gloating rapture viewed the ore,
    And his pleased avarice gave the willing nod;   70
They reach the ship, the freshening breezes rise,
And smooth and fast they speed beneath the moonlight skies.

What heart e'er felt more ardent longings now?
    What eye than his e'er beamed with riper hope,
As curbed impatience on his open brow   75
    There painted fancy's unsuspected scope?
As all that's fair the foreign land appeared,
By ever-present love, wonder and hope endeared.

Meanwhile through calm and storm, through night and day,
    Unvarying in her aim the vessel went,   80
As if some inward spirit ruled her way
    And her tense sails were conscious of intent,
Till Albion's cliffs gleamed o'er her plunging bow,
And Albion's river-floods bright sparkled round her prow.

65 on] *possibly* oer *in Esd.*

Then on the land in joy Kathema leaped,   85
    And kissed the soil in which his hopes were sown—
These even now in thought his heart has reaped.
    Elate of body and soul he journeyed on,
And the strange things of a strange land passed by
Like motes and shadows pressed upon his charmèd eye.   90

    Yet Albion's changeful skies and chilling wind
        The change from Cashmire's vale might well denote:
    There Heaven and Earth are ever bright and kind,
        Here blights and storms and damp for ever float,
    Whilst hearts are more ungenial than the zone,—   95
Gross, spiritless, alive to no pangs but their own.

    There flowers and fruits are ever fair and ripe,
        Autumn there mingles with the bloom of spring,
    And forms unpinched by frost or hunger's gripe
        A natural veil o'er natural spirits fling,—   100
    Here woe on all but wealth has set its foot,
Famine, disease and crime even Wealth's proud gates
        pollute.

    Unquiet death and premature decay,
        Youth tottering on the crutches of old age,
    And, ere the noon of manhood's riper day,   105
        Pangs that no art of medicine can assuage,
    Madness and passion, ever mingling flames,
And souls that well become such miserable frames—

    These are the bribes which Art to man has given,
        To yield his taintless nature to her sway: 110
    So might dark night with meteors tempt fair Heaven
        To blot the sunbeam and forswear the day,
    Till gleams of baleful light alone might show
The pestilential mists, the darkness and the woe.

Kathema little felt the sleet and wind,   115
   He little heeded the wide-altered scene;
The flame that lived within his eager mind
   There kindled all the thoughts that once had been;
He stood alone in England's varied woe,
Safe, 'mid the flood of crime that round his steps did flow.   120

It was an evening when the bitterest breath
   Of dark December swept the mists along
That the lone wanderer ⟨came to⟩ a wild heath.
   Courage and hope had stayed his nature long;
Now cold and unappeased hunger spent   125
His strength; sensation failed in total languishment.

When he awaked to life cold horrors crept
   Even to his heart, for a damp deathy smell
Had slowly come around him while he slept.
   He started—lo, the fitful moonbeams fell   130
Upon a dead and naked female form
That from a gibbet high swung to the sullen storm!

And wildly in the wind her dark hair swung,
   Low mingling with the clangour of the chain,
Whilst ravenous birds of prey that on it clung   135
   In the dull ear of night poured their sad strain,
And ghastlily her shapeless visage shone
In the unsteady light, half mouldered to the bone.

Then madness seized Kathema, and his mind
   A prophecy of horror filled; he scaled   140
The gibbet which swung slowly in the wind
   High o'er the heath.—Scarcely his strength availed
To grasp the chain when, by the moonlight's gleam,
His palsied gaze was fixed on Zeinab's altered frame.

123 ⟨came to⟩ *conjecture for smudged words*   133 her *apparently, over* its
138 to *possibly* thro *in Esd.*

Yes!—in those orbs once bright with life and love   145
    Now full-fed worms bask in unnatural light;
That neck on which his eyes were wont to rove
    In rapture, changed by putrefaction's blight,
Now rusts the ponderous links that creak beneath
Its weight, and turns to life the frightful sport of death.   150

Then in the moonlight played Kathema's smile
    Calmly—in peace his spirit seemed to be.
He paused, even like a man at ease awhile,
    Then spoke: 'My love! I will be like to thee,—
A mouldering carcase or a spirit blest,—   155
With thee corruption's prey or Heaven's happy guest!'

He twined the chain around his neck, then leapt
    Forward,—in haste to meet the life to come . . .
An iron-souled son of Europe might have wept
    To witness such a noble being's doom,   160
As on the death-scene Heaven indignant frowned.
And night in horror drew her veil the deed around.

For they had torn his Zeinab from her home,—
    Her innocent habits were all rudely riven
And, dragged to live in love's untimely tomb,   165
    To prostitution, crime and woe was driven;
The human race seemed leagued against her weal
And indignation cased her naked heart in steel.

Therefore against them she waged ruthless war
    With their own arms of bold and bloody crime;   170
Even like a mild and sweetly-beaming star
    Whose rays were wont to grace the matin–prime
Changed to a comet, horrible and bright,
Which wild careers awhile then sinks in dark-red night.

164–6 *See n.*   164 riven] shriven *Esd.*   172 rays *above* [beams] grace
above [mark]   173 changed to *above* [Even like]

Thus, like its God, unjust and pitiless,   175
    Crimes first are made and then avenged by Man.—
For where's the tender heart whose hope can bless
    Or Man's or God's unprofitable plan,—
A universe of horror and decay,
Gibbets, disease and wars and hearts as hard as they?   180

50

THE RETROSPECT

CWM ELAN, 1812

To trace Duration's lone career,
To check the chariot of the year,
Whose burning wheels forever sweep
The boundaries of oblivion's deep,—
To snatch from Time the monster's jaw   5
    The children which she just had borne
And, ere entombed within her maw,
    To drag them to the light of morn,
And mark each feature with an eye
Of cold and fearless scrutiny! . . .   10
It asks a soul not formed to feel,
An eye of glass, a hand of steel,
Thoughts that have passed and thoughts that are
With truth and feeling, to compare
A scene which wildered fancy viewed   15
In the soul's coldest solitude,
With that same scene when peaceful love
Flings rapture's colour o'er the grove,

177 hope *above* [heart]
TITLE, AUTOGRAPH, TEXT: *Esd.* DATE: *See n.* PRINTED: *15–end, Dowden,*
Life, 1886.
    4 deep,—] deep . . . *Esd.*   10 scrutiny! . . .] scrutiny . . . *Esd.*   14
feeling,] feeling *Esd.*   compare] compare; *Esd.*

When mountain, meadow, wood and stream
With unalloying glory gleam,   20
And to the spirit's ear and eye
Are unison and harmony.

The moonlight was my dearer day;
Then would I wander far away,
And, lingering on the wild brook's shore   25
To hear its unremitting roar,
Would lose in the ideal flow
All sense of overwhelming woe;
Or at the noiseless noon of night
Would climb some heathy mountain's height,   30
And listen to the mystic sound
That stole in fitful gasps around.
I joyed to see the streaks of day
Above the purple peaks decay,
And watch the latest line of light   35
Just mingling with the shades of night;
For day with me was time of woe
When even tears refused to flow;
Then would I stretch my languid frame
    Beneath the wild-wood's gloomiest shade,   40
And try to quench the ceaseless flame
    That on my withered vitals preyed;
Would close mine eyes and dream I were
    On some remote and friendless plain,
And long to leave existence there,   45
    If with it I might leave the pain
That with a finger cold and lean
Wrote madness on my withering mien.

It was not unrequited love
That bade my wildered spirit rove;   50
'Twas not the pride disdaining life,
That with this mortal world at strife

22–23 *Esd. has a space between these lines. No space in 1886*

Would yield to the soul's inward sense,
Then groan in human impotence,
And weep because it is not given　　　55
To taste on Earth the peace of Heaven.
'Twas not that in the narrow sphere
　　Where Nature fixed my wayward fate
There was no friend or kindred dear
　　Formed to become that spirit's mate,　　　60
Which, searching on tired pinion, found
Barren and cold repulse around;
Ah, no! yet each one sorrow gave
New graces to the narrow grave.

For broken vows had early quelled　　　65
The stainless spirit's vestal flame;
Yes! whilst the faithful bosom swelled,
Then the envenomed arrow came,
And Apathy's unaltering eye
Beamed coldness on the misery;　　　70
And early I had learned to scorn
　　The chains of clay that bound a soul
Panting to seize the wings of morn,
And where its vital fires were born
　　To soar, and spurn the cold control　　　75
Which the vile slaves of earthly night
Would twine around its struggling flight.
Oh, many were the friends whom fame
Had linked with the unmeaning name
Whose magic marked among mankind　　　80
The casket of my unknown mind,
Which hidden from the vulgar glare
Imbibed no fleeting radiance there.
My darksome spirit sought—it found
A friendless solitude around.　　　85

77–78 *Esd. has no space. A space in 1886*

For who that might undaunted stand,
The saviour of a sinking land,
Would crawl, its ruthless tyrant's slave,
And fatten upon Freedom's grave,
Though doomed with her to perish, where   90
The captive clasps abhorred despair.

They could not share the bosom's feeling,
Which, passion's every throb revealing,
Dared force on the world's notice cold
Thoughts of unprofitable mould,   95
Who bask in Custom's fickle ray,
Fit sunshine of such wintry day!—
They could not in a twilight walk
Weave an impassioned web of talk,
Till mysteries the spirit press   100
In wild yet tender awfulness,
Then feel within our narrow sphere
How little yet how great we are!
But they might shine in courtly glare,
Attract the rabble's cheapest stare,   105
And might command where'er they move
A thing that bears the name of love;
They might be learnèd, witty, gay,
Foremost in fashion's gilt array,
On Fame's emblazoned pages shine,   110
Be princes' friends, but never mine!

Ye jagged peaks that frown sublime,
Mocking the blunted scythe of Time,
Whence I would watch its lustre pale
Steal from the moon o'er yonder vale: 115

Thou rock, whose bosom black and vast,
    Bared to the stream's unceasing flow,
Ever its giant shade doth cast
    On the tumultuous surge below:

100 spirit *Esd.*] spirits *1886*

Woods, to whose depth retires to die   120
The wounded Echo's melody,
And whither this lone spirit bent
The footstep of a wild intent:

Meadows, whose green and spangled breast
These fevered limbs have often pressed,   125
Until the watchful fiend Despair
Slept in the soothing coolness there!—
Have not your varied beauties seen
The sunken eye, the withering mien,
Sad traces of the unuttered pain   130
That froze my heart and burned my brain?

How changed since Nature's summer form
Had last the power my grief to charm,
Since last ye soothed my spirit's sadness,
Strange chaos of a mingled madness!   135
Changed?—not the loathsome worm that fed
In the dark mansions of the dead,
Now soaring through the fields of air,
And gathering purest nectar there,
A butterfly, whose million hues   140
The dazzled eye of wonder views,
Long lingering on a work so strange,
Has undergone so bright a change!

How do I feel my happiness?
I cannot tell, but they may guess   145
Whose every gloomy feeling gone,
Friendship and passion feel alone;
Who see mortality's dull clouds
    Before affection's murmur fly,
    Whilst the mild glances of her eye   150
Pierce the thin veil of flesh that shrouds
    The spirit's radiant sanctuary.

121 Echo's *1904*] echo's *Esd., 1886*   146 feeling *over* [passion]   152
radiant *Esd.*] inmost *1886*

O thou! whose virtues latest known,
First in this heart yet claim'st a throne,—
Whose downy sceptre still shall share   155
The gentle sway with virtue there,—
Thou fair in form, and pure in mind,
   Whose ardent friendship rivets fast
The flowery band our fates that bind,
   Which incorruptible shall last   160
When duty's hard and cold control
Had thawed around the burning soul,—
The gloomiest retrospects that bind
With crowns of thorn the bleeding mind,
The prospects of most doubtful hue   165
That rise on Fancy's shuddering view
Are gilt by the reviving ray
Which thou hast flung upon my day.

51

THE WANDERING JEW'S SOLILOQUY

? 1810–11

Is it the Eternal Triune, is it He
Who dares arrest the wheels of destiny
   And plunge me in this lowest Hell of Hells?
Will not the lightning's blast destroy my frame?
   Will not steel drink the blood-life where it swells?   5
   No—let me hie where dark Destruction dwells,
To rouse her from her deeply-caverned lair,
And, taunting her cursed sluggishness to ire,
   Light long Oblivion's death-torch at its flame
And calmly mount Annihilation's pyre.   10

∧ 164 crowns *above* [coronets]   bleeding *above* the mind   *caret after* the
153–68 *For punctuation see Notes.*
∨ TITLE, AUTOGRAPH, TEXT: *Esd.*   DATE: *See n.*   PRINTED: *From Esd., Bertram
Dobell, with* The Wandering Jew, *1887.*
  3 this *Esd.*] the *1887*   10–11 *Esd. has a blank space; no space in 1887*

Tyrant of Earth! pale Misery's jackal Thou!
   Are there no stores of vengeful violent fate
   Within the magazines of Thy fierce hate?
No poison in Thy clouds to bathe a brow
   That lowers on Thee with desperate contempt?   15
Where is the noonday Pestilence that slew
   The myriad sons of Israel's favoured nation?
Where the destroying Minister that flew
   Pouring the fiery tide of desolation
Upon the leagued Assyrian's attempt?   20
Where the dark Earthquake-daemon who engorged
At thy dread word Korah's unconscious crew?
Or the Angel's two-edged sword of fire that urged
Our primal parents from their bower of bliss
   (Reared by Thine hand) for errors not their own   25
   By Thine omniscient mind foredoomed, foreknown?
Yes! I would court a ruin such as this,
   Almighty Tyrant, and give thanks to Thee!—
   Drink deeply, drain the cup of hate, remit!... Then I may die!

52

SONNET

TO IANTHE [SHELLEY]

September 1813

I love thee, baby! for thine own sweet sake;
   Those azure eyes, that faintly dimpled cheek,
   Thy tender frame so eloquently weak,
Love in the sternest heart of hate might wake;

/\ 22 thy *Esd.*] the *1887*   27 this, *1887*] this *Esd.*   28 Tyrant,]
Tyrant! *Esd., 1887* Thee!–] thee.–*Esd.,* Thee – *1887*   29 deeply,] deeply–
Esd., 1887 hate,] hate–*Esd.,* hate; *1887* remit!... Then I] remit then I *Esd.,*
remit this—I *1887*
   *At the end of this poem Shelley notes the last of a series of line-counts which run
through Esd. His total is 2822.*

\/ TITLE, AUTOGRAPH, TEXT, DATE: *Esd.*   PRINTED: *Dowden, Life, 1886.*

But more when o'er thy fitful slumber bending   5
   Thy mother folds thee to her wakeful heart,
Whilst love and pity, in her glances blending,
   All that thy passive eyes can feel impart;
More, when some feeble lineaments of her
   Who bore thy weight beneath her spotless bosom,   10
As with deep love I read thy face, recur,—
   More dear art thou, O fair and fragile blossom;
Dearest when most thy tender traits express
The image of thy mother's loveliness.

53

SONNET

EVENING—TO HARRIET [SHELLEY]

September 1813
Probably composed 31 July 1813

O thou bright Sun, beneath the dark blue line
   Of western distance that sublime descendest,
And, gleaming lovelier as thy beams decline,
   Thy million hues to every vapour lendest,
And over cobweb lawn and grove and stream   5
   Sheddest the liquid magic of thy light,
   Till calm Earth, with the parting splendour bright,
Shows like the vision of a beauteous dream!—
   What gazer now with astronomic eye
Could coldly count the spots within thy sphere?   10
   Such were thy lover, Harriet, could he fly
The thoughts of all that makes his passion dear,
   And, turning senseless from thy warm caress,
   Pick flaws in our close-woven happiness.

TITLE, AUTOGRAPH, TEXT: *Esd.*   DATE: *Esd., but seen n.*   PRINTED: *Dowden,*
Life, 1886.
  13 from *above* [to]

54

TO HARRIET [SHELLEY]

May 1814

Thy look of love has power to calm
   The stormiest passion of my soul;
Thy gentle words are drops of balm
   In life's too bitter bowl;
No grief is mine, but that alone   5
These choicest blessings I have known.

Harriet! if all who long to live
   In the warm sunshine of thine eye,
That price beyond all pain must give
   Beneath thy scorn to die—   10
Then hear thy chosen own too late
His heart most worthy of thy hate.

Be thou, then, one among mankind
   Whose heart is harder not for state,
Thou only virtuous, gentle, kind   15
   Amid a world of hate;
And by a slight endurance seal
A fellow-being's lasting weal.

For pale with anguish is his cheek,
   His breath comes fast, his eyes are dim,   20
Thy name is struggling ere he speak,
   Weak is each trembling limb;
In mercy let him not endure
The misery of a fatal cure.

TRANSCRIPT: *Harriet Shelley in Esd.* TITLE, DATE, TEXT: *Esd.* PRINTED: *Dowden, Life, 1886.*

   7 Harriet] *Harriett here and in the title: not in accordance with her normal spelling or Shelley's.*

   After line 18, at the foot of the page, Harriet has added Cook's Hotel

To Harriet —

Thy look of love has power to calm
The stormiest passion of my soul,
Thy gentle words are drops of balm
In life's too bitter bowl;
No grief is mine, but that alone
These choicest blessings I have known.

Harriet! if all who long to live
In the warm sunshine of thine eye,
That price beyond all pain must give,
Beneath thy scorn to die —
Then hear thy chosen own too late
This heart most worthy of thy hate.

Be thou then one among mankind
Whose heart is harder not for state,
Thou only virtuous, gentle, kind,
Amid a world of hate;
And by a slight endurance seal
A fellow being's lasting weal

Cooke's Hotel

Harriet Shelley's transcript, in the Esdaile Notebook, of poem No. 54. (*See p. 110*)

Oh, trust for once no erring guide!   25
    Bid the remorseless feeling flee;
'Tis malice, 'tis revenge, 'tis pride,
    'Tis anything but thee;
Oh, deign a nobler pride to prove,
And pity if thou canst not love.   30

55

'FULL MANY A MIND ...'
[See Appendix]

56

TO HARRIET [? GROVE]
Undated

Oh, Harriet, love like mine that glows
    What rolling years can e'er destroy?
Without thee can I tell my woes?
    And with thee can I speak my grief?

Ah no,—past all the futile power   5
    Of words to tell is love like mine;
My love is not the fading flower
    That fleets ere it attain its prime:
A moment of delight with thee
    Would pay me for an age of pain.   10

I'll tell not of rapture and joy
    Which swell through the libertine's frame;
That breast must feel bliss with alloy
    That is scorched by so selfish a flame.

TRANSCRIPT: *Harriet Shelley in Esd.*   TEXT: *Esd.*   TITLE, DATE: *See n.*

It were pleasure to die for my love,   15
  It were rapture to sink in the grave
My eternal affection to prove,
  My ever dear Harriet to save.

Without thee all pleasure were gloom
  And with thee all sorrow were joy;   20
Ere I knew thee, my Harriet, each year
  Passed in mournful rotation away,—
No friend to my bosom was dear,
  Slow rolled the unvarying day.

Shall I wake then those horrors anew   25
  That swelled in my desperate brain
When to Death's darkened portals I flew
  And sought misery's relief to my pain?

That hour which tears thee from me
  Leaves nothing but death and despair,   30
And that, Harriet, never could be
  Were thy mind less enchantingly fair.

'Tis not for the charms of thy form
  Which decay with the swift-rolling year,—
Ah, no! Heaven expands to my sight—   35
  For Elysium with Harriet must be!

57

'LATE WAS THE NIGHT...'
[See Appendix]

24 unvarying] unvayraying *Esd.*   28 misery's] miseries *Esd.*   35
Written below, still in H. Shelley's hand,
          Cwm Elan / Adieu my love good night. *See n.*

58

TO ST. IRVYNE—TO HARRIET [GROVE]

28 February 1805

O'er thy turrets, St. Irvyne, the winter winds roar,
    The long grass of thy towers streams to the blast;
Must I never, St. Irvyne, then visit thee more?
    Are those visions of transient happiness past?

When with Harriet I sat on the mouldering height,   5
    When with Harriet I gazed on the star-spangled sky,
And the August moon shone through the dimness of night,—
    How swiftly the moments of pleasure fled by!

How swift is a fleeting smile chased by a sigh
    This breast, this poor sorrow-torn breast must confess;   10
Oh Harriet, loved Harriet, though thou art not nigh,
    Think not thy lover thinks of thee less!

How oft have we roamed, through the stillness of eve,
    Through St. Irvyne's old rooms that so fast fade away!
That those pleasure-winged moments were transient I
      grieve: 15
    My soul like those turrets falls fast to decay.

My Harriet is fled, like a fast-fading dream,
    Which fades ere the vision is fixed on the mind,
But has left a firm love and a lasting esteem
    That my soul to her soul must eternally bind.   20

When my mouldering bones lie in the cold, chilling grave,
    When my last groans are borne o'er Strood's wide lea,
And over my tomb the chill night-tempests rave,
    Then, loved Harriet, bestow one poor thought on me.

TRANSCRIPT: *Harriet Shelley in Esd.*   TITLE: *See n.*   DATE, TEXT: *Esd.*

811450   I

APPENDIX

POEMS NOT BY SHELLEY OR OF
DOUBTFUL AUTHORSHIP

43

FRAGMENT OF A POEM

THE ORIGINAL IDEA OF WHICH
WAS SUGGESTED
BY THE COWARDLY AND INFAMOUS BOMBARDMENT
OF COPENHAGEN

Before January 1811

The ice-mountains echo, the Baltic, the Ocean,
   Where cold sits enthroned on its solium of snow;

AUTHOR: *Elizabeth Shelley. See Intr. § 2.*   AUTOGRAPH: *Esd. Pf.*   DATE: *See n.*
TITLE, TEXT: *Esd.*   PRINTED: *From Pf., Hogg, Life, 1858.*

   *The Pf. version consists of 4 stanzas of which the first and third correspond,
apart from a few variations, with stanzas II and I respectively of the Esdaile
version. Its second and fourth stanzas are as follows*
          Old Ocean to shrieks of Despair is resounding
            It washes the terror-struck nations with gore
          Wild horror the fear-palsied Earth is astounding
            And murmurs of fate fright the dread-convulsed shore.
            The Andes in Sympathy start at the roar
          Vast Etna alarmed leans his flame-glowing brow
          And huge Teneriffe stoops with his pinnacled snow.

          All are Bretheren,—   the African bending
            To the stroke of the hard hearted Englishmans rod,
          The courtier at Luxury's Palace attending,
            The Senator trembling at Tyranny's nod
            Each nation wch kneels at the footstool of God
          All are Bretheren; then banish Distinction afar
          Let concord & Love heal the miseries of War!

   For a complete, literal transcript of Pf. see Kenneth Neill Cameron, Shelley and
His Circle, *ii. 701–3*

Even Spitzbergen perceives the terrific commotion,
   The roar floats on the whirlwinds of sleet as they blow;
   Blood clots with the streams as half-frozen they flow, 5
Lurid flame o'er the cities the meteors of war,
And mix their deep gleam with the bright polar glare.

Yes! the arms of Britannia victorious are bearing
   Fame, triumph, and terror wherever they spread;
Her Lion his crest o'er the nations is rearing,—   10
   Ruin follows—-it tramples the dying and dead.
   But her countrymen fall—the blood-reeking bed
Of the battle-slain sends a complaint-breathing sigh:
It is mixed with the shoutings of victory.

I see the lone female,—the sun is descending,   15
   Dank carnage-smoke sheds an ensanguining glare,—
Night its shades in the orient earlier is blending,
   Yet the light faintly marks a wild maniac's stare,—
   She lists to the death shrieks that came on the air,
The pride of her heart to her bosom she prest,   20
Then sunk on his form in the sleep of the blest.

45

'COLD ARE THE BLASTS...'

1808

Cold are the blasts when December is howling,
   Chill are the damps on a dying friend's brow,—
Stern is the Ocean when tempests are rolling,
   Sad is the grave where a brother lies low;

AUTHOR: *Elizabeth Shelley. See Intr. § 2.* AUTOGRAPH: *Esd. Pf.* DATE, TITLE, TEXT: *Esd.* PRINTED: *From Pf., Hogg,* Life, *1858.*
   The Esd. version of this poem is a variant of the third poem in Original Poetry by Victor and Cazire, *the joint work of Shelley and his sister Elizabeth, published*

But chillier is scorn from the false one that loved thee,   5
More stern is the sneer from the friend that has proved thee,
More sad are the tears when these sorrows have moved thee,
    That envenomed by wildest delirium flow.

And alas! thou, Louisa, hast felt all this horror,—
    Full long the fallen victim contended with fate,   10
Till, a destitute outcast, abandoned to sorrow,
    She sought her babe's food at her ruiner's gate.
Another had charmed the remorseless betrayer,
He turned laughing away from her anguish-fraught prayer,—
She spoke not but, wringing the rain from her hair,   15
    Took the rough mountain path though the hour was late.

On the cloud-shrouded summit of dark Penmanmawr
    The form of the wasted Louisa reclined;
She shrieked to the ravens loud-croaking afar,
    She sighed to the gusts of the wild-sweeping wind:—   20
'Ye storms o'er the peak of the lone mountain soaring,
Ye clouds with the thunder-winged tempest-shafts lowering,
Thou wrath of black Heaven, I blame not thy pouring,
    But thee, cruel Henry, I call thee unkind!'

Then she wreathed a wild crown from the flowers of the
        mountain,   25
    And deliriously laughing the heath-twigs entwined,
She bedewed it with tear drops, then leaned o'er the fountain,
    And cast it a prey to the wild-sweeping wind.
'Ah, go!' she exclaimed, 'where the tempest is yelling,
'Tis unkind to be cast on the sea that is swelling,   30
But I left, a pitiless outcast, my dwelling;
    My garments are torn—so, they say, is my mind.'

in 1810. The Pf. version represents an attempt by Shelley to write out from memory, for Hogg's benefit, some samples of Elizabeth's composition. It consists of the 5 Esdaile stanzas together with broken passages, adding up to some 14 lines, taken from Victor and Cazire, xii and xiii; there are considerable verbal variants. For a literal transcription see Kenneth Neill Cameron, Shelley and His Circle, ii. 625–7.

Not long lived Louisa, and over her grave
    Wave the desolate limbs of a storm-blasted yew;
Around it no demon or ghosts dare to rave,   35
    But spirits of love steep her slumbers in dew.
Then stay thy swift steps 'mid the dark mountain heather,
Though bleak be the scene and severe be the weather,
For perfidy, traveller, cannot bereave her
    Of the tears to the tombs of the innocent due.   40

55

'FULL MANY A MIND...'

1815

Full many a mind with radiant genius fraught
    Is taught the dark scowl of misery to bear,—
How many a great soul has often sought
    To stem the sad torrent of wild despair!

It would not be Earth's laws were given   5
    To stand between Man, God and Heaven,—
To teach him where to seek and truly find
    That lasting comfort, peace of mind.

AUTHOR: *? Harriet Shelley.* TRANSCRIPT: *Harriet Shelley in Esd.* DATE, TEXT:
Esd. PRINTED: *Louise S. Boas,* Harriet Shelley, *1962.* *Under line 8*
Harriet has written Stanmore 1815.

'LATE WAS THE NIGHT . . .'

Undated

Late was the night, the moon shone bright;
  It tinted the walls with a silver light,
And threw its wide, uncertain beam
  Upon ⟨ ?its⟩ rolling mountain stream.

That stream so swift that rushes along   5
  Has oft been ⟨ ?dyed⟩ by the ⟨murderers'⟩ song,
It oft has heard the exulting wave
  Of one who oft the ⟨murderers⟩ braved.

The Alpine summits which, raised on high,
  Peacefully frown on the valley beneath   10
And lift their huge forms to the sky
  Oft have heard the voices of death.

Now not a murmur floats on the air,
  Save the distant sounds of the torrent's tide,
Not a cloud obscures the moon so fair,   15
  Not a shade is seen on the rocks to glide.

See, that fair form that [?none] ⟨ ?can save⟩;
  Her garments are tattered her bosom so bare,—
She shrinks from the yawning, watery grave,
  And, shivering, around her enwraps her dark hair. 20

Poor Emma has toiled o'er many a mile,
  The victim of misery's own sad child,
Pale is her cheek, all trembling awhile,
  She totters and falls on the cold-stricken wild.

AUTHOR: *? Harriet Shelley.*   TRANSCRIPT: *Harriet Shelley in Esd.*   TEXT: *Esd.*
DATE: *See n.*
  4 the] its *Esd.*   6 murderers'] murderes *Esd.*   8 murderers] murderes
Esd.   5–8, 17 *See n.*

NOTES ON THE TEXT

P. 1, No. 1. To Harriet [Shelley]. *Title*: As given by Shelley in 1813, 'To Harriet'. On account of Shelley's satisfaction when a piratical publisher omitted the poem Mary Shelley omitted it from *PW 1839*. In *PW 1840* she restored it with the title 'To Harriet * * * * *'.

Version I, 5–8 ⎫ A notable early example of Shelley's fusion of
Version II, 5–8 ⎭ personal and humanitarian love.

P. 2, No. 2. A Sabbath Walk. *Date*: The 'winter's day' (l. 28) and the 'mountain labyrinth' (l. 5) suggest Shelley's stay at Keswick, Nov. 1811 to Feb. 1812. The Tremadoc period, a year later, is a possibility, but fits less with the mood and the events. The poem seems to recall Southey's 'Written on Sunday Morning' (1797).

9: Shelley's social and religious resistance was always of the kind deriving from thwarted 'devotedness', the antithesis of natural anarchy or atheism. For the early conflict of 'devotedness' with unattractive forms of worship cf. Rimbaud, 'Les Premières Communions'. For Shelley's habit of alternative recourse to 'the wilds' cf., in 1819, the 'Ode to the West Wind'. See N. Rogers, *Shelley at Work*, pp. 211–29.

P. 4, No. 3. The Crisis. *Date*: Possibly the period of strong God-winian influence following Shelley's expulsion from Oxford.

These Sapphic stanzas are so arranged in the Notebook as to be both preceded and followed by a pair of poems in loose unrhymed Southeyan stanzas. The dactylic kick in its fourth line made the Sapphic stanza a lively one for political verse-writing, cf. Canning's 'Needy Knife-Grinder', published in *The Anti-Jacobin*, 1798. For its use in 18th-century prophecies of doom, cf. Cowper's 'Lines Written During a Period of Insanity' and Isaac Watts's 'The Day of Judgment'.

P. 5, No. 4. Passion. *Title*: Incomplete in *Esd*. In a memorandum owned by Lord Abinger, Dowden comments: 'Some flower whose name Shelley had forgotten or did not know.' The poem, however, does not hang on identification of the flower. What matters is the meaning of 'Passion'. For Shelley, and many of his period, this frequently meant something like 'enthusiasm together with driving power': something like the *Tätigkeit* or *Wirksamkeit* which is the concern of characters in Goethe. With this goes a notion of devotedness, cf. above, 'A Sabbath Walk'. The important thing was to control 'passion', and not be controlled by it: otherwise the 'Essence of Virtue' would become a poison. This fits with Godwin's tenet that crime and goodness spring from like causes. Perhaps the best comment is in *Hamlet* III. ii. 65–70. Sexual passion is relevant only in so far as it affects the driving power of the creative artist, philosopher, or reformer: cf. 'The Triumph of Life', 275, and No.

50, 'The Retrospect' below, lines 93 and 147. *Date*: See the following n., and n. on No. 1 above.

6–10: cf. Wordsworth, 'A Poet's Epitaph', 5–8, which had appeared in *Lyrical Ballads*, 1798. Shelley's interest in Wordsworth was stimulated by Southey at Keswick. See n. on No. 2, above.

P. 7, No. 5. To Harriet [Shelley].

15–20: The remembrance of Harriet and her death haunted Shelley as long as he lived, and Mary even afterwards. In these lines, written while he loved her, there is pathos, irony, and a reminder both of his sea-visions at Lerici and of the preoccupation with drowning which appears in, e.g., 'Stanzas Written in Dejection near Naples', the 'Ode to Liberty', and *Adonais*.

P. 8, No. 6. Falsehood and Vice. *Date*: Possibly the period of *Posthumous Fragments of Margaret Nicolson*, where the macabre humour suggests a kinship; the missed opportunities for Necessitarian treatment seem to place the poem before the Godwinian impetus (cf. No. 3, above). C. D. Locock suggests that an impetus came from 'Fire, Famine and Slaughter', Coleridge's 'War Eclogue'. The general terminology of monarchs, tyrants, superstition, luxury, fetters, liberty, slavery, and war-mongering owes much to Erasmus Darwin, poet of *The Botanic Garden*, *The Temple of Nature*, &c, which Shelley enjoyed, and in which his interest was aroused by Darwin's close associate Dr. Lind, his Platonic mentor at Eton. The following lines [*T. of Nature*, IV. 84–85, 507–8] are typical:

> There the curst spells of Superstition blind,
> And fix her fetters on the tortured mind . . .
> Fierce furies drag to pains and realms unknown
> The blood-stain'd tyrant from his tottering throne.

Like Praed and other Etonians Shelley had early fluency with the octosyllabic couplet; with these cruder beginnings cf. the ease and beauty of, e.g., 'Lines Written in the Euganean Hills'.

40: GOLD, MONARCHY and MURDER: Shelley's capitalization is a reminder of the phrase 'blood and gold' of which he later made symbolic use. cf. *The Mask of Anarchy*, 65; 'Charles I', i. 61; 'Lines on Hearing of the Death of Napoleon Bonaparte', 35; and see Rogers, *Shelley at Work*, 280 foll.

P. 12, No. 7. To the Emperors, Etc. *Date*: Between the battle of Austerlitz and the Godwinian impetus (see nn. on Nos. 3 and 6, above): once again Shelley misses Necessitarian openings in his subject. For the influence of Erasmus Darwin see n. on No. 6.

1: *Coward chiefs* . . . : cf. Lucretius, *De Rerum Natura*, ii. 5–6:

> Suave etiam belli certamina magna tueri
> Per campos instructa, tua sine parte pericli . . .,

which Shelley quoted among the Notes to *Queen Mab* [v. 58].

P. 14, No. 8. To NOVEMBER. Shelley's association of Harriet with Nature is a reminder of his feeling in *Queen Mab* that

> the flame
> Of consentaneous love inspires all life (viii. 107–8).

It was this feeling, partly Lucretian but also instinctive, which later combined with his intellectual revulsion to free him from the doctrine of Necessity.

P. 15, No. 9. WRITTEN ON A BEAUTIFUL DAY IN SPRING. *Title*: The title and idea may connect with Wordsworth's 'Lines Written in Early Spring', but the manner is eighteenth-century, with the variations of line-length then loosely thought 'Pindaric'. *Date*: See nn. on Nos. 2 and 4.

18: The bathetic last line contains an idea better expressed later in the 'Ode to the West Wind': 'If Winter comes, can Spring be far behind?' As a step from these early crudities towards the Ode may be noted the quotation among the Notes to *Queen Mab* [v. 4–6] from *Iliad* vi. 146 foll., οἵη περ φύλλων γενεή, τοιήδε καὶ ἀνδρῶν . . . .

P. 16, No. 10. ON LEAVING LONDON FOR WALES. *Date*: The reference to Snowdon, and the poem generally, seem to fit the autumn of 1812 better then Shelley's visit to Cwm Elan in the previous year. For the influence of Erasmus Darwin see n. on No. 6.

19: *Hail to thee* . . .: Shelley is here the disciple of Rousseau, seeking virtue among unspoiled people and places. There would seem to have been psychological repetition in his excursion to Switzerland with Mary in 1816. See Rogers, *Shelley at Work*, 40 foll. Cf. nn. on No. 50, below.

P. 18, No. 11. A WINTER'S DAY. *Date*: The 'cascades' (l. 4) and the 'moor' (l. 12) again suggest the winter at Keswick, 1811–12, though Tremadoc, in the following winter, is again a possibility.

8 foll.: For Shelley's reactions to Nature see notes on Nos. 2, 4, 8, 10, above, and cf. his remark to Peacock in a kindred connexion (letter of 6 Nov. 1818): 'I always seek in what I see the manifestation of something beyond the present and tangible object.'

26–27: Syntactically unrelated to what precedes: evidently miscopied or misremembered.

P. 20, No. 12. To LIBERTY. *Date*: Conjecturable as falling within the period of Godwinian influence (see n. on No. 3, above), and having some relation to the note of nos. 31 and 32. For the influence of Erasmus Darwin see n. on No. 6.

11–14: There seems to be a note from Bunyan's hymn, 'He who would valiant be . . .'.

26 foll.: Dowden noticed the influence of Campbell's 'Ye Mariners of England' and 'The Battle of the Baltic'. The Shelleyan victory, however, will be achieved not by Nelson's cheerful sailors but by the operation of Necessity in the Universe.

46: Necessity, again, rather than love and Intellectual Beauty, as later, will bring about this Shelleyan paradise.

P. 22, No. 13. On Robert Emmet's Tomb. *Title*: Printed by Dowden and others as 'On Robert Emmet's Grave'. *Date*: From the visit of Shelley and Harriet to Dublin, February–March, 1812. See Shelley's letter to Miss Hitchener, April 16, 1812.

Robert Emmet (1778–1803) was executed by the British after the failure of his attempt to revive the 'United Irishmen' movement. He could have escaped to America but stayed to await an answer from Sarah Curran, to whom he had proposed marriage. Thomas Moore wrote of the incident in his well-known laments, 'He is far from the land' and 'O breathe not his name'. Shelley writes in the metre made popular by Moore, a forgotten merit of which is that when used, as Moore often used it, for the composition of words to fit tunes it loses its jingle and is wonderfully adaptable alike to 4/4, 3/4, or 6/8 time. Sarah Curran was the daughter of J. P. Curran, and sister of Amelia Curran, who painted the unfinished portrait of Shelley now in the National Portrait Gallery.

12: Syntax demands 'and silently weeping as he passes'. Metre prevents emendation.

P. 23, No. 14. A Tale of Society, Etc. *Date*: *Esd.* has '1811', but in Shelley's letter to Elizabeth Hitchener of 7 Jan. 1812 (*Pf.*) the poem is described as 'the overflowings of the mind this morning'. This may be just an attempt to give actuality. See n. on line 37. The comparatively hopeless outlook of the poem is in accordance with Godwin's doctrine in *Political Justice* that the best life the peasant can lead is that of virtue. If he achieve it he 'is in a certain sense happy . . . he is happier than a stone'. Once again something is owed to Wordsworth. For the influence of Erasmus Darwin see n. on No. 6.

15: *lingering from/to*: Either preposition both fuses and extends two *OED* meanings of the verb, 'to stay on in a place, esp. from reluctance to leave it' and 'to continue barely alive'.

19: Here and in line 26 I have preferred the *BM* reading as giving a better sense and possibly correcting memory.

37: The row of crosses might be taken as suggesting that *BM*, in turn, has suffered from a lapse of memory.

P. 28, No. 16. The Monarch's Funeral.

6: Probably refers to George III, who became ill and incapable late in 1810; cf. Shelley's sonnet of 1819, 'An old mad, blind, despised and dying king . . .'. A Regency Act was passed in January 1811.

45–52: Since the vocative 'Pride' must go with the imperative 'restore' it has seemed best to bring it closer in effect by treating Shelley's exclamation mark as one of his anticipatory ones (see Introduction, § 5). The syntactical extension of this same abstract noun to provide a vocative for 'feel' (lines 49, 52) is awkward, but has been helped, I hope, by my forward-pointing dash after the exclamation mark (45).

57–58: Cf. *Q. Mab.* ix. 31–32.

> Yon monarch, in his solitary pomp,
> Was but the mushroom of a summer day.

Both passages look back to Darwin's description in *The Botanic Garden* of how 'when a Monarch or a mushroom dies' the apparently dead mass soon teems with life. See n. on No. 6.

P. 31, No. 17. TO THE REPUBLICANS OF NORTH AMERICA. *Title/Date*: Shelley (*Esd.*) wrote 'South' and changed this to 'North', though there is more accuracy in Rossetti's *1870* title, 'The Mexican Revolution', taken from *BM*, where (14 Feb. 1812) Shelley sends Miss Hitchener his 'tribute' to the insurrection of the priest Miguel Hidalgo. This had happened in 1810, but the news seems fresh to him.

P. 33, No. 18. WRITTEN AT CWM ELAN, 1811. *Date*: Shelley's correspondence shows he was at Cwm Elan from *c.* 9 July to *c.* 4 Aug. The unusual metre is suggestive of 'Stanzas—April, 1814', 12–24, and *Prometheus Unbound*, i. 774 foll.

15: *tangèd*: an archaism cognate with the noun 'tang', a form of 'tongue', used in the sense of the 'projecting part of an instrument' and involving 'the strong ringing note when any large bell or any sonorous body is suddenly struck with force'. See *OED*.

P. 34, No. 19. TO DEATH. *Date*: See Hogg, *Life*, i. 124. The Pf. manuscript was given to Hogg by Shelley at Oxford. The poem has a certain metrical interest. Out of such beginnings in what the eighteenth century called 'Pindarics' grew Shelley's later ode-forms and chorus-forms. See n. on No. 9.

1⎫
5⎭ Cf. 1. Corinthians xv. 55.

29: cf. 'Hymn to Intellectual Beauty', 36.

63–68: The conclusion is somewhat marred by the point that the 'victory' is won not by a victor but by a process, Necessity, to which the poet seems to offer submission and defiance at the same time.

P. 37, No. 20. 'DARK SPIRIT OF THE DESERT RUDE . . .'. *Date*: The gloomy tone and the Necessitarian note seem to fit Shelley's 1811 visit to Cwm Elan better than his return there with Harriet in 1812. See n. on No. 18, above.

45–46: Syntax requires 'Suck'st . . . decay'st' or 'To suck . . . to decay'. Rhyme, sound, and metre prevent emendation.

P. 38, No. 21. [REALITY]. *Title/Date*: The poem marks a movement towards Platonism and away from both Godwinian and 'Gothic' gloom. 'On Death', Mary Shelley's title, *1839*, just misses the Platonic point.

Epigraph: Unlike most of Shelley's epigraphs this asserts something which the poem challenges rather than something he is himself asserting.

10: *light*: Shelley's revision of 10–12 goes with the light-and-darkness imagery of lines 25–30 to anticipate the Platonic symbolism found in *Prometheus Unbound, Adonais,* and in his maturer poetry *passim.* Together with the Platonic concept of the immortality of thought, which Shelley substituted for Christian immortality, we have (l. 7) the faith in Man's endurance which is also a keynote in *Prometheus Unbound.*

P. 40, No. 22. 'DEATH-SPURNING ROCKS . . .'. *Date*: Possibly deducible from Shelley's visit to the Valley of Rocks, Lynton, when he was in Devonshire: see letter to Godwin, 5 July 1812. If, however, Cwm Elan was the scenic background the mood of the poem seems fitted to his 1811 visit rather than to his 1812 one.

P. 41, No. 23. THE TOMBS. *Date*: From Shelley's visit to Dublin in 1812.
   21–25: Defective sense is probably due, as elsewhere, to mistakes of memory or copying. The reference is to the suppression of Wolfe Tone's rebellion of 1798.

P. 42, No. 24. TO HARRIET [SHELLEY].
   25 foll.: In this, the most mature of the Harriet poems, Shelley approaches the language and ideas both of Shakespeare's Sonnets and of his own *Epipsychidion.*
   32–52: The syntax is defective in *Esd., 1886, & edd.*
   40: Sc. 'bringing out all the fire . . .'.
   42: *holy friendship*: Shelley's mood here is working its way towards the Platonic idea of a purified feeling, beyond Ἔρως. This eighteenth-century usage, perhaps coloured from German Hellenism, did not lack warmth. Nelson wrote to Lady Hamilton as 'My dear friend . . .', and Benjamin Franklin, as a widower, dreamed of 'my friend the former Mrs. Franklin'. cf. No. 50, 158, where on the warmth of 'ardent friendship' hangs the meaning of the poem, from its title to its climax.
   61–65: The language has some affinity with *Hellas,* 197–200 and 795–6.

P. 45, No. 25. SONNET: TO HARRIET [SHELLEY].
   2: *somewhat*: See *OED* for instances of the substantival usage.

P. 45, No. 26. SONNET TO A BALLOON LADEN WITH *KNOWLEDGE. Title*: Shelley's underlining of the last word makes plain that it means 'political instruction'. This and the following poem anticipate whimsically his later plans for a steam-boat service as a means of carrying enlightenment. See N. Rogers, *Shelley at Work,* 93 foll. *Date*: From Shelley's visit to Devonshire and his dating in *Esd.* of No. 32.

P. 46, No. 27. SONNET ON LAUNCHING SOME BOTTLES, ETC. *Title/Date*: See No. 26.
   8: *her West*: The United States, thought of by Shelley as a land of Liberty. Hutchinson's capital neatly makes the point.

P. 47, No. 28. SONNET ON WAITING FOR A WIND, ETC. *Date*: See n. on No. 26, above.

P. 48, No. 29. To Harriet [Shelley].
    25–29: See n. on No. 1, 5–8, above.

P. 49, No. 30. Mary to the Sea-Wind. *Title*: Not necessarily connected with the Mary of Nos. 37–40. *Date*: Uncertain, but the unusual metre and movement suggest that it belongs to a late part of the period covered by the Esdaile Poems, and the 'Sea Wind' suggests Shelley's period in Devonshire.

P. 50, No. 31. A Retrospect of Times of Old. *Date*: From its Necessitarian kinship with *Queen Mab* and with the next poem, which is dated in *Esd*.

Once again a poem falls flat from the dullness of a triumph over tyranny which is due to a process rather than human effort; even the high-sounding names in lines 71–72 do not help this, and the last two lines must represent the climax in Shelley of Godwin's 'happier-than-a-stone' philosophy. See above, nn. on No. 14. In 'Ozymandias' the feeling is similar, but it is humanized by the triumphant dramatization.

    1–13: Sntax unpointed in MS, apart from the misplaced bracket.
    8, 25: Cf. Erasmus Darwin, *Economy of Vegetation*, iv. 67–68
            . . . the Simoon rides the tainted air,
            Points his keen eye, and waves his whistling hair.
Cf. Coleridge, 'Religious Musings', 268, which comes closer to Darwin than Shelley does, and which Shelley could have known: 'through the tainted noon/The simoon sails'. See n. on No. 6.

P. 53, No. 32. The Voyage. Metre probably influenced by Southey's *Thalaba*. The Necessitarian motif of the poem is grafted on to the enthusiasm of contemporary writers for archaeological discovery. Shelley had read Volney's *Les Ruines*, and its information about Palmyra appears in *Queen Mab*.

    2: *horrent*: Lat. *horrentem*, 'bristling with fear', but also 'fear-inspiring'. Cf. *Queen Mab*, vi. 132; *Hellas*, 283.
    68: The nautical superstition that whistling could bring a wind appears in a manuscript of 'The Boat on the Serchio'. See N. Rogers, 'Shelley's Text' in the *Times Literary Suppt.*, 10 Aug. 1951. Cf. M. R. James's famous ghost-story 'Oh, whistle! And I'll come to you my Lad'.

P. 62, No. 33. A Dialogue. Shelley's *Note*: the quotation is from *Queen Mab*, iii. 80–83.

P. 66, No. 35. 'Hopes that Bud . . .'
    5: *blossoms*: Perhaps it was because of 'flowers' in the next line that, in *Pf.*, Shelley preferred the pretty 18th-century Latinism 'honours', printed by Hogg. Cf. Vergil, *Georgics* ii. 405, and Jebb's beautiful version of Tennyson, 'Tithonus', 1: 'Marcescunt nemorum, nemorum labuntur honores.'
    15–20: Shelley's row of crosses in *Pf.* seems an acknowledgement that his memory was merely substituting something. Cf. n. on No. 14, 37.

P. 68, Nos. 37–40. FOUR POEMS FOR MARY. *Advertisement*: by Shelley: The 'many [poems] written' may not include No. 30, below, but probably include 'To Mary Who Died in This Opinion'. The 'friend' is Hogg; 'Leonora' was the title of a novel which he and Shelley planned. The quotation from St. Augustine ('I was not yet in love and wanted to be in love: I was seeking something to love, liking [the idea of] loving') was used as an epigraph for *Alastor*. The passage well sums up the kind of sensitivity that Professor Notopoulos (*The Platonism of Shelley*, 14–15) has called 'natural Platonism'.

37. 21–24: The 'voyage symbol', frequently used for escape by travel (cf. No. 10) or the exportation of knowledge and enlightenment (cf. Nos. 26, 27, 28), could also stand for death (cf. *Adonais*, 487–95). Frequently the last involved suicide; cf. Southey's thought, expressed in 1793 to Horace Bedford, of 'seeking happiness in France, America or the grave'. Though these three forms of emigration were more commonly talked of than practised, the fashion may have left some impression on Harriet Shelley and Fanny Imlay.

The reference in Shelley's cancelled footnote to 'Romances of Leadenhall St.' concerns the trashy novels published by the Minerva Press.

P. 74, No. 41. [BIGOTRY'S VICTIM].

10: *desert/desart*: With this interesting evidence that two manuscripts can differ in the same passage cf. the not uncommon belief that Shelley's misspellings have significance, more especially the attempts of H. Buxton Forman to argue that he used *desart* as noun and *desert* as adjective. See N. Rogers, 'Shelley's Spelling: Theory and Practice', *Keats–Shelley Memorial Bulletin* ed. D. Hewlett, No. xvi, 1965.

P. 75, No. 42. [LOVE AND TYRANNY]. Probably concerned with Shelley's feelings for Harriet Grove.

P. 79, No. 46. HENRY AND LOUISA.

21–22: The gaps seem to indicate that something is lacking in Shelley's memory or his documents.

140–3: Probably some miscopying. *Tho* looks possible for the first word.

153–4: Syntax uncertain, but the aposiopesis seems dramatically likely.

159: *mixed . . . urge*: Vergil's *immixti* or *commixti . . . urgent*; urge here meaning 'continue to press on with'.

166–75: The syntax is obscure and the only manuscript punctuation is the comma in line 166.

166: *the Genius of the South*: An echo probably of Southey, 'To the Genius of Africa'.

168–70: Cf. Erasmus Darwin, *Loves of the Plants*, iii. 441–4
   E'en now in Afric's groves with hideous yell
   Fierce SLAVERY stalks, and slips the dogs of hell;
   From vale to vale the gathering cries rebound,
   And sable nations tremble at the sound.

172: *varied*: Used in the sense of the Latin *varius* = 'many-coloured' involving the idea of 'ever-changing': cf. No. 16, line 10, and No. 50, line 128.

189: cf. n. on 49: 68.

214 foll.: The description follows Erasmus Darwin's account (*Loves of the Plants*, iii.) of a distraught lady named Eliza who seeks her husband on the battlefield of Minden: with line 233 cf. Darwin (l. 263) 'So wings the wounded deer her headlong flight'.

260: In a note to Book X of *Thalaba the Destroyer* Southey mentions a statue 'like that of Memnon, from which proceeded a small sound and a pleasant noise when the rising sun came, by his heat, to rarify and force out, by certain small conduits, the air which in the cool of the night was condensed within it'. Memnon, son of Eos and Tithonus, was a mythical king of Ethiopia.

P. 92, No. 47. A TRANSLATION OF THE MARSEILLAISE HYMN. *Date*: Shelley's letter of *c.* 19 June 1811 seems integrated with the stanza there quoted.

Though Shelley had yet to attain his full excellence as a translator this version is remarkable for its insensitiveness both to the original words and to the tune. Possibly it is a versifying, or re-versifying, of some other English version.

5. 6: Bouillé was a royalist general.

P. 95, No. 48. WRITTEN IN VERY EARLY YOUTH. *Date*: Perhaps the age of 15 might mark the beginning of 'very early youth'; perhaps certain reminders of Gray's *Elegy Written in a Country Churchyard* might be a reason for connecting the poem with Shelley's version in Latin Sapphics, ascribed by Medwin to 1808–9.

P. 96, No. 49. ZEINAB AND KATHEMA. *Date*: In June 1811 Shelley read and was much impressed by Miss Owenson's *The Missionary*, of which the influence is noticeable in this poem.

13–24: The syntax, running across the stanzas is awkward and hard to improve by punctuation. The stops ending lines 17 and 18 are what appear to be Shelley's.

68: An early example of Shelley's occasionally abrupt metrical variety. The missing foot and the ellipsis of 'of gold' require a pause suggesting 'heap [*sc.*] of dirt'. He is seldom *un*metrical, though cf. 46. 189 above.

163 foll.: With the change of one word this could be summarized as Godwin summarized the ground-plot of his novel *Caleb Williams*: '. . . atrocious crime, committed by a [woman] previously of exemplary habits'.

164–6: 'Shriven', in *Esd.* must be a miscopying. Otherwise the meaning is clear, despite a syntactical fusion, which leaves 'habits' without its second verb and 'was driven' without a subject.

P. 102, No. 50. THE RETROSPECT, ETC. *Date*: Part of manuscript title. Shelley put a full-stop after 'Retrospect', but to notice this would be to prefer a point in the manuscript to the point of the poem, which is a looking-backward in terms of both place and time. *Metre*: Here, better than anywhere else among the Esdaile poems, Shelley foreshadows his mastery of the octosyllabic couplet.

1–10: The syntax is loose but just intelligible if treated as exclamatory rhetoric ending in an aposiopesis; the latter may be marked by the preservation, for once, of Shelley's three-dot stop, strengthened by an exclamation mark. If preserved at line 4 it would halt the rhetoric, which needed, instead, to be speeded by a comma plus dash.

11–22: 'It' (line 11) refers to 'to compare' (line 14); 'asks' has three objects, 'An eye . . .', 'a hand . . .', 'Thoughts . . .'. The object of 'compare' is 'A scene' (line 15). The comparison 'With that same scene' (line 17), which is the whole point of the 'retrospect', would disappear if we allowed Shelley's semi-colon after line 14.

79: *name* i.e. the question-begging name of 'atheist'.

86 *who* = 'those who'.

153–68: A good example of the long, complex periods which Shelley left others to clarify by punctuation, cf. above, Preface pp. viii–ix and Introduction §5. In lines 153–4 he seems to have telescoped two constructions, 'O thou . . . [who] claim'st . . .' and 'O thou! whose virtues . . . [claim] . . .'; cf. his syntactical confusion in No. 20, 45–46. But the comma placed by Dowden at the end of line 153 indicates that 'whose virtues latest known' is an absolute, participial construction on the model of the Genitive Absolute in Greek and the Ablative Absolute in Latin. The meaning is 'O thou! who, thy virtues being latest known' (i.e. 'more recently than those of Harriet Grove'). The difficulty, smoothed out by Dowden's judicious comma, arises from the brachylogy whereby Shelley leaves his reader to deduce out of the genitive 'whose' a subject for the verb 'claim'st'.

Taken as a whole the 16 lines construct as follows:

A. The vocative, 'O thou!', invoking Harriet Shelley.
B. Two subordinate clauses qualifying A:
    1. 'whose . . . throne'.
    2. 'Whose . . . sceptre . . . shall . . . share / The sway . . . there'.
C. A reiteration of the vocative 'Thou', picked up from A, and strengthened by the qualifying phrases 'fair . . . mind'.
D. A third subordinate clause, 'whose . . . band', qualifying C.
E. A fourth subordinate clause, picking up the word 'band' from D and qualifying it. (N.B. 'our fates that bind' is an inversion for 'that our fates bind'.)
F. A fifth subordinate clause, 'Which . . . last', again picking up and qualifying 'band' in E.
G. A sixth subordinate clause, 'When . . . soul', picking up the verb 'last' from F and qualifying it.
H. First subject of the main sentence, 'The . . . retrospects'.
I. A seventh subordinate clause, 'that bind . . . mind', qualifying H.
J. Second subject of the main sentence, 'The prospects', asyndetonically co-ordinated with H and qualified by the phrase 'of . . . hue'.

K. An eighth subordinate clause, 'That . . . view', qualifying the co-ordinated subjects, H and J, of the main sentence.

L. The verb of the main sentence, 'Are', required by the co-ordinated subjects H and J.

M. The complement, 'gilt', required by L.

N. A phrase, 'by . . . ray', qualifying M.

O. A ninth subordinate clause, picking up 'ray' from N and qualifying it.

The hinge comes at lines 162–3, where the preliminary concatenation of subordinate clauses is joined to the beginning of the main sentence. Dowden put a semicolon here; Hutchinson's comma plus dash, which seems to look both backward and forward, was a great improvement. The effect in Hutchinson's edition is spoiled, however, by a comma plus dash after 'view' at the end of line 166. This has two effects. First it separates the co-ordinated subjects, 'retrospects' and 'prospects', from their verb and its complement, 'Are gilt'. Secondly, the words between these two strong stops are turned by them into a compartment which upsets the whole meaning of the passage. Hutchinson, who did not have the manuscript before him, is not to be blamed; here too Dowden had put a semicolon, so, allowing for the possibility of some parallelism justified by the manuscript, he repeated his own stop at the end of line 162. To make the passage finally clear we must allow lines 165–8 to run unstopped to their end.

As often elsewhere, the whole point of the poem lies in the force of what the syntax has to convey, which is that in Harriet Shelley's love ('ardent friendship', 158) her husband's 'gloomiest retrospects' and his 'most doubtful prospects' are turned alike to warmth and gold.

For Shelley's use of 'friendship', cf. n. to No. 24, 42, above.

P. 107, No. 51. THE WANDERING JEW'S SOLILOQUY. Medwin gives, divergently, '1808' and '1809' as the date when Shelley was first drawn to this subject. The style suggests a later date.

16: Shelley seems to fuse recollection of the pestilence in 1. Chronicles, xxi with the language of Psalms, xci 6.

20: cf. Byron, 'The Destruction of Sennacherib', and 2. Kings, xviii–xix.

22: cf. Numbers, xvi.

28–29: The whole poem depends on a rhetorical pause of some sort between the prayer contained in the three final imperatives and the clause indicating the consummation so devoutly wished by the Jew. The confused meaning of line 29, as hitherto printed, is partly due to Dobell's reading, 'this' and partly due to uncritical acceptance of a manuscript punctuation destructive of the syntax in which the meaning has to be sought.

P. 109, No. 53. SONNET, EVENING, ETC. *Date*: At head of manuscript, 'Sep. 1813;' underneath, 'July 31, 1813'. Probably composed on the earlier date and, with the preceding poem, copied out on the later one.

P. 111, No. 56. To HARRIET [? GROVE]. *Title/Date*: The manuscript date, 'May 1813', probably represents Harriet Shelley's transcription. Shelley is quite unlikely to have written anything so immature that year. The verses are so far below his standards of 1810–13 that the question arises whether they date from an early time when the 'Harriet' was Harriet Grove. The words added below need not link them with either of Shelley's visits to Cwm Elan; it is not impossible that they could have been left there by Harriet Grove when visiting her relatives, found by Harriet Shelley, and transcribed by her—speculation might further consider whether this could have been under a belief that she herself was their 'Harriet'. The 'my Harriet' of line 18 is, of course merely a common extension of the 'ethical' usage, and not, as has been suggested to me, an indication that Shelley's wife is referred to.

Perhaps there has been a conflation of two poems, the first ending at line 10.

P. 113, No. 58. To ST. IRVYNE, ETC. *Title*: Dowden suggests that this may have been taken from the name of the owner of an estate in the neighbourhood of Field Place: Lady Irvyne. Strood (22) is a near-by village.

NOTES ON THE APPENDIX

P. 114, No. 43. FRAGMENT OF A POEM, ETC. *Date*: *Pf.*, a letter to Hogg, is dated '11 Jan. 1811'. With lines 1–2 of its fourth stanza cf. No. 17, *passim*, and No. 27, 5–8, and n. Softer hearts and rods might be accessible in the Land of Liberty, though the problem of the African, like that of Shelley's bottles, might be to survive the voyage.

P. 115, No. 45. 'COLD ARE THE BLASTS . . .'. Versifying of this kind, traceable to 'Gothic' romances and translations, may be due partially to the influence, often circuitous, of 'Ossian'. There are affinities between these lines and the passages of 'Ossian' translated into German by Werther, just before his suicide.

12: '*She sought her babe's food at her ruiner's gate*': An anticipation of the ballad 'Young Parson Richards' written by Shelley in 1819 (Julian Ed. iii. 152).

P. 118, No. 57. 'LATE WAS THE NIGHT . . .'. *Date*: *Esd.* has '1815', but this must refer to the date of the transcription by Harriet Shelley. If, as seems likely, she was the author, no date can be conjectured.

5–8: If, as might be, the rhyme words in 6–7 have been reversed, perhaps the first 'murderes' in *Esd.* is a miscopying for 'murderous'; perhaps 'wave' should be 'waves' and 'braved' 'braves'; perhaps the second 'murderes' should be 'murderer'. Even so, the sense would seem to defy conjecture.

17: The last two words are just yielded by *Esd.*; if we assume that the first letter is a capital, that the last has lost its ink, and that some such subject for the verb as 'none' has been omitted.

INDEX OF TITLES

INDEX OF FIRST LINES